"Great, insightful book. This book is right on with the values it discusses. It really exposes the myths and societal pressures on teens when they are dating. As a high schooler, I now have a better understanding of how to date and what not to do when dating."

- from an online review

"Wow! I wish I had this guide when I was growing up! . . . provides a direct, clear, personal, and very readable guide to developing fulfilling, honest, deeply satisfying love relationships based upon biblical truth."

- from an online review

"He makes the point that understanding yourself and your relationship to Jesus Christ is the basis for eventually being able to have a truly effective and satisfying life including relationships."

- from an online review

"So true - what we need is love - real love. Without an intimate relationship with God, we don't have real love in our hearts so it isn't there to give - it will always be a corrupted version that we learn from our parents, friends, previous relationships, magazines, TV, music, and so on. Only God's love is true and pure - and when we cultivate a relationship with Him then we experience His love to know for ourselves and to give to others. Everything else is a miserable copycat out for self . . . I see so many young girls selling themselves short in the name of acceptance and love. They are looking in all the wrong places - places that will leave deep wounds that will cause pain for years to come. If I only knew then what I know now. If anything, I've learned from all my screw-ups is just how perfect, powerful and amazing the love of God is."

- comment posted online in response to reading Chapter 17

i

"This book can help a person find something that can't be bought - true love."

"It's amazing how little preparation most people do to get ready for dating. It's almost like they don't realize that when they date, who they date, and how they date will have a lot to do with whether or not they'll one day find true love and have a lifelong loving marriage."

"Many people make dating choices mainly based upon liking someone, feelings, and looks. It's no wonder that so many people eventually get their heart broken and only about 6% of marriages end up lasting 50 years."

Straight Talk About Teen Dating

If I'd only known the truth about . . .

A guide to dating from a Christian perspective for pre-teens and teens

Second Edition

James Wegert, M.Ed.
School Counselor

Strong Book Publishing
Lancaster, PA

This book is dedicated to my beloved Pam - without her love and support this book would not have been possible.

ISBN-13: 978-1460983843

Printed and bound in the United States of America.

ATTENTION YOUTH GROUPS, CHURCHES, ETC.: This book is being studied by youth groups and Sunday School classes - some leaders/teachers assign one or two chapters to read one week and then have discussion the following week, while others just read the chapters together each week and then have discussion. To make the book affordable to study, discounts are available on bulk orders - please see p. 133 for the bulk order form. A copy of this book is available free upon request to pastors, youth pastors, Sunday School teachers, youth group leaders, etc. who are considering studying it by sending an email to TLLinfo@aol.com.

Table of Contents

Prologue

Many people read the prologue of a book to decide whether or not it's worth reading. If you decide not to read it, this could be my only opportunity to communicate some crucial, possibly even life changing, information to you. So let me summarize some suggestions that I explain later in the book . . .

If you go on the journey of preparing yourself for dating by learning when, who, and how to date - you're more likely to have a lifelong loving Christian marriage

The first step toward finding a person with whom you could have a lifelong loving Christian marriage is to become the type of person that God wants you to date - a keeper

You should only date a keeper and it's best to find a way to get to know someone before dating them

Sadly, many teens use the disastrous "Dating without God" approach to dating in which dating choices are mainly based upon whether someone likes them, they like someone, feelings, and looks - they start dating before they're ready - and they choose to date people that God doesn't want them to date

Broken hearts from broken relationships are a major source of emotional pain and anguish in our society

The huge number of broken hearts can be reduced if more teens fully prepare themselves for dating, if they're spiritually and emotionally ready before dating, if they're very selective about who they date, if they pay more attention to danger signs during dating, and if they don't get emotionally attached too quickly during dating

Dating should be a slow process in which you discover what the person you're dating is really like and whether or not God wants you to be married to this person for the rest of your life

Long make out sessions and sex before marriage makes it more likely that you'll become emotionally attached to someone that God doesn't want you to become emotionally attached to (please see pp. 62-66 before you decide that this statement doesn't make any sense)

Having sex before marriage can be harmful to you and to your future - contrary to popular belief, most teens aren't doing it

True love is much more than just the feeling of being "in love", it's supposed to be a lifelong commitment - it almost never fails

True love alone isn't a good enough reason to get married

The decision to get married is a really big decision in your life - it should be made only after careful consideration and prayer

Many people marry before they're ready to be married - often with disastrous results; statistics show that waiting to get married until at least age 24 significantly decreases the likelihood of divorce

Developing and keeping the feeling of being "in love" at a high-level during dating is relatively easy, but keeping it at a high-level during marriage requires a lot of effort

Divorce doesn't "just happen" - it's caused by many things such as selfishness, unrealistic expectations, one or both people not having true love for the other, unwillingness to make the effort on a daily basis to try to meet the needs of your husband or wife and to keep the feeling of being "in love" at a high level, uncaring words and actions, a desire to control your husband or wife, unwillingness to grow up, addictions, poor communication, out of control spending

The most exciting, most fulfilling, and most joyous marriage on earth is a lifelong loving Christian marriage

I hope that you decide to read this book to start the journey of preparing yourself for dating!

- James Wegert

Introduction

"Why should I take the time to read this book? I'm busy!"

This book has two big goals. The first one is to help you to prepare yourself for dating. The second one is to help reduce the number of broken hearts and the divorce rate in our society by starting a cultural revolution in regard to the approach to dating that most people use (more about that later).

In order to achieve these goals, I'm going to give you information/suggestions about dating and things related to dating from a Christian perspective that I wish I'd known when I was a teen. I developed this material using the large number of bad choices that I've made in my life, the bad choices that I've seen many others make in their lives, my education, and research.

This book was written to make a difference in your life. It's going to give you a point of view on teen dating that you've probably never heard before and information about an approach to dating that you've probably never heard of. As you read the book, at times you may feel like yelling and tearing it to pieces. My request is that you take the time to read it from cover to cover, even if you don't agree with some of the information. Please use what makes sense to make it more likely that you'll have a lifelong loving marriage if you choose to get married one day. Please forgive me in advance for being overly blunt at times.

For those of you who have the "I pretty much know it all, I don't need to read any book" attitude, please read Chapter 23 first before it's too late.

This book wasn't designed to be read once and then forgotten - it was designed to be referred back to over and over again - think of it as a guide or a roadmap for dating. Isn't it a good idea to have a map before you go on a road (dating) that you've never been on before, that you haven't been on long, or that you're lost on?

Look around you - many romantic relationships between men and women aren't healthy. Countless teens are dating before they're ready and are making dating choices mainly based upon whether they like someone, feelings, and looks - instead of only dating a hard-working person with Godly character. Some teens are in an emotionally and/or physically abusive dating relationship and they don't understand that the foundation of any healthy relationship is mutual respect. The number of couples living together without being married is at an all-time high. Huge numbers of people are marrying too quickly, for the wrong reasons, without true love, and without much thought. Many people marry with a selfish "as long as I feel in love" commitment instead of an "as long as we both shall live" commitment. Millions of people are unhappy because they don't have the loving fulfilling marriage relationship that they hoped for. Many couples don't feel "in love" as much as they used to feel. The divorce rate is way too high and sadly the divorce rate for Christian couples isn't much different from the rate for non-Christian couples.

These facts are proof that we aren't doing enough to motivate teens to go on the journey of preparing themselves for dating.

I hope that this book will help you to paint a picture in your mind of how wonderful a lifelong loving Christian marriage could be . . . and that by picturing it; you'll be motivated to go on the journey.

The journey of preparing yourself for dating is going to take a good deal of effort and learning as well as spiritual, personal, and emotional growth. Although it won't be easy, the possible rewards if you decide to get married one day are great - rewards like having a husband or wife:

- with whom you have a close loving relationship

- who's your best friend

- who treats you with kindness, tenderness, love, and respect in their thoughts, words, and actions on a daily basis

- who loves you unconditionally just the way you are

- who tries their best to meet your emotional, physical, social, and financial needs

- who consistently makes the effort to keep the feeling of being "in love" at a high level (explained later)

- who's faithful to you no matter what

- with whom you can resolve differences in a calm constructive caring manner

- who wants only the best for you

- with whom you have the feeling of being "in love" (most of the time)

- who has true love for you (a lifelong commitment)

- who you have true love for

- with whom you can share the blessing of children

- with whom you can have a forty, fifty, or sixty-year fulfilling marriage with which God is well pleased

To jumpstart you on the journey of preparing yourself for dating, I'm going to share with you many things that I wish I'd known during my teenage years. I admit that I don't have all of the answers and that I'm still learning, but my hope is that this information will help you to avoid the mistakes that I've made and that I've seen so many others make.

I could have avoided so much heartache and mental anguish if I'd only known the truth about . . .

Notes:

1

. . . our society having lots of people with serious problems

"Carefully use dating to find out if serious problems exist"

As a teenager, I didn't fully realize that our society has lots of people who have some type of serious problem. I mistakenly thought that most people were raised in a home like mine - a home in which they were given firm, fair, kind, and consistent discipline by parents who loved them. Little did I know that there were many parents who didn't really care about being a good parent, who didn't know that permissive parenting (letting their child pretty much do whatever they feel like doing) makes it more likely that their child will develop a serious problem, or who didn't have the parenting skills and/or the strength needed to bring up their children right.

When parents don't fulfill their responsibilities, it has a negative effect upon their children and on generations to come. Children who don't learn about Christian faith, integrity, honesty, concern and respect for others, what true love is, selflessness, how to spend money wisely, and the importance of hard work usually don't know how to raise their children well and the cycle continues to the next generation.

Violence, greed, selfishness, alcohol and other drug abuse, premarital sex, having children without being married, divorce - all of these things in our society today could be significantly reduced if more parents did a good job of fulfilling their responsibilities.

You might be saying to yourself, "What does all of this information have to do with teen dating?" Teen dating can possibly lead to marriage one day and it's very important for your sake that you don't end up marrying a person who has one or more serious problems. Unfortunately, many people who have serious problems (such as selfishness, dependency, anger, untreated mental health issues, disrespect toward others, irresponsibility, lack of integrity, dishonesty, laziness, careless spending, a desire to control you, an unwillingness to grow up, and addictions to alcohol, other drugs, pornography, gambling, etc.) will try to hide their problems from you during the dating process. They'll make every effort to only show you their good side. When humans have the feeling of being "in love" and they're dating a person who seems to have everything that they're looking for (looks, personality, money, etc.) - they usually ignore or minimize the importance of serious problems, problems that often destroy a marriage. If you end up marrying a person with a serious problem, your life could become a living hell. For example, if you marry a person who has a hidden anger problem, almost always their hidden anger will eventually come out on you. It happened to me (more about that later).

The purpose of this chapter is to warn you that many people who seem to have it all together have hidden serious problems that you need to try to discover before dating and during dating. Please don't set yourself up for disaster by sugarcoating or overlooking a serious problem in the person who you're dating (for example, by saying to yourself what I've heard over and over again from people I counsel - something like, "Yes it's true that he can't get along with lots of people including his mother, but he's *so* nice to me - and that's all that matters").

Reflection: What are the dangers of dating someone who has a serious problem?

2

. . . living in a war zone with people who are brainwashed

"The forces of evil want your heart and mind for their own gain"

When I was your age, I didn't realize that I was living in a war zone with people who were brainwashed. Yeah, I know it sounds crazy, like I'm out of my mind - but I'm completely serious. And the war zone today is even more dangerous now than it was then.*

The war zone I'm talking about isn't like the one you see in the movies or on TV with guys shooting at each other - it's a war zone in your heart and mind between the forces of good and the forces of evil. (I know it still sounds a bit wacko, but hear me out.)

It's crucial for you to understand that you're being bombarded by evil influences that want to control your heart and mind. For example, the content of many magazines, books, movies, the internet, TV shows, and music isn't pleasing to God. They glamorize materialism, swearing, alcohol and other drug use, violence, lust, and sex before marriage. I realize that things from the media may be exciting to read, watch or listen to for the moment, but you need to know that they damage your heart and mind. This is especially true for males who watch or see garbage, because they can visualize what they have seen for a long, long time - it's almost as if it gets permanently burned into their brain. Sadly, if I want to, I can still visualize one of the first pornographic pictures that I was shown by a "friend" when I was in fifth or sixth grade. So don't believe anyone who says, "Yeah, I look at, watch, and listen to that stuff - but it doesn't have any effect on me." They're fooling themselves. (Research shows that how the brain works negatively changes when pornography is viewed on a regular basis.)

The truth is that God doesn't want you to fill up your head with garbage. You need to know that the reason so much garbage is being produced by the media is because garbage sells. Do you understand that many people are trying to put garbage into your head in order to make money? In other words, they're trying to take advantage of you for their own personal gain. They know that the value systems of many teenagers aren't solidly formed. They're trying to impose their evil value system upon you. They want to deceive you into thinking that bad choices are OK and fun - so they'll be able to sell you more garbage in the future. They could care less about you as a person and the negative effect that watching or listening to their garbage has upon your heart and mind.

In regard to brainwashing - the definition of brainwashing is something like, "forcing someone to have certain attitudes or beliefs." Do you think that the constant daily barrage of the media has brainwashed many people into thinking that things like pornography; having sex before marriage, drinking, and gambling are OK? Contrast what the media says to what God says in Philippians, chapter 4; verse 8; 1 Corinthians, chapter 6, verse 18-20; and Ephesians, chapter 5, verse 18. The media has a way of making things that are clearly sinful to God and that will damage or destroy your life, seem like harmless fun.

I urge you to take whatever steps that are necessary throughout your life to protect your heart and mind from the negative influence of the media (which means that you need to limit what you hear and see - for example, refuse to read books and magazines, listen to music, watch TV shows, or go to movies that glamorize sin). Don't be fooled into thinking that the media "doesn't have any effect on me."

Unfortunately, it seems that many of us have also been brainwashed by the media and our popular culture to believe that there's only one approach to dating. The message that we receive relentlessly every day is that when a person wants to start dating all they need to do is use the approach of searching for a person with looks, personality, and possibly money who they like, who they have feelings for, who they are attracted to - so that they can "fall in love" with them. Since we see people start romantic relationships using this approach over and over again in movies and on TV, hear about romantic relationships using this approach all the time in secular music, read about people using this approach in books and magazines, and see our friends starting romantic relationships using this approach (and so far it seems to be working) - we really believe the fairy tale that all we have to do is search for a person who has everything we want and be ready to "fall in love and live happily ever after." I made the mistake of using this approach.

Unfortunately, this approach has several major problems. The first problem is that it's based upon selfishness - can you see it? A person using this approach is just trying to get what they want for themselves. The second problem is that the result of using this approach is usually heartbreak. In fact, over the past one hundred years, the number of broken hearts from using this approach is in the billions - and sadly even after having their heart broken, most people use the same approach again and again simply because they don't know what else to do. The third problem with this approach is that it promotes that being lazy is OK - it basically says that a person doesn't have to do much of anything to prepare themselves for dating - just be searching and be ready because "you never know when you're going to fall in love." Doesn't this approach sound a lot like gambling? In fact, part of its allure is that it's kind of mysterious and exciting. But just like gambling, the odds of winning (having a lifelong loving marriage) by using this approach are stacked against you. People are rolling the dice by making dating decisions without really thinking and hoping that the dice don't come up "snake eyes" (divorce).

But the biggest problem with this approach is that it doesn't include God. In fact, let's call this disastrous approach what it is - it's "Dating without God." Isn't it unbelievably sad that so many people use an approach to dating that's based upon a fairy tale, selfishness, laziness, that's a lot like gambling, that rarely works, and that doesn't include God?

Hopefully all of us can agree that doing anything without God isn't a good thing - and this includes "Dating without God."

There must be an alternative to "Dating without God" - and there is. I realize that the name isn't clever, but let's just call the alternative approach to dating, "Dating with God." Doesn't it make sense to use an approach to dating that fully includes God - someone who loves us unconditionally and who will help us to make good choices throughout the dating process?

The "Dating with God" approach to dating is explained in Chapters 10 through 16.

*Please see p. 117 for information about a book that explains this "battlefield" in more detail.

<u>Reflection:</u> How have the media and the popular culture influenced your planned approach to dating or the approach to dating that you're currently using?

At a family reunion I had the opportunity to talk privately with a twenty-something relative who was distraught about his break up with a longtime girlfriend. After I empathetically listened to him share the pain of his broken heart as he stared at the floor, I decided to take the risk of asking him the very important question, "Was God a part of your relationship?" He paused, possibly because he was surprised by the question. He then lifted his head up, looked me in the eye and said "no." I then spent a good amount of time explaining the highlights of the "Dating with God" approach to dating to him. He politely listened to what I had to say but sadly, even after a broken heart and our talk, I found out later that he had decided to continue using the "Dating without God" approach. He has yet to find true love.

Notes:

Question: *Why is it so difficult to find a "good" man and why is it so difficult to find a "good" woman (with "good" being defined as a hard-working person with Godly character) to date?*

Frankly, my opinion is that our society just isn't producing enough "good" men and "good" women. I believe that one of the reasons for this is that we're not doing a good enough job of teaching teens how to live their lives for Christ as well as teaching them the many benefits of living their lives for Christ - both now and eternally. We're letting the false popular culture message that selfishness is the way to happiness/fulfillment drown out the gospel message that loving God and loving others is the only lasting way to happiness/fulfillment. With God's help, my hope is that this book will help to produce more "good" men and "good" women by communicating crucial information to teens including the fact that living their lives for Christ is better than living their lives for personal gain and personal pleasure.

"Every person is a unique treasure created by God, more valuable than silver or gold - even if they don't have fame, fortune, or looks - regardless of what anyone says, does, or thinks."

3

. . . divorce devastating our society

"People who say that divorce is no big deal simply don't know what they're talking about"

During my teenage years I didn't think much about divorce. It didn't seem to happen very often and when it did, it wasn't talked about. Man, have times changed - for the worse. Everywhere you go and from the media, you hear about people getting divorced. Divorce, something that used to be rare, is now commonplace. Now it's almost accepted as something that's "no big deal", that's "OK", that "just happens", and that "there's nothing we can do about it."

It's true that divorce has become a pandemic in our society. I didn't know what a pandemic was until I looked it up in the dictionary - it said, pandemic: something affecting a very high number of people. The statistics out there are a bit confusing - but most sources seem to agree that at least 30% of all marriages (almost one in three) end in divorce. That sounds very high to me.

Let's put it this way, if divorce was a disease, and 30% of all married people caught it, do you think that we'd be sitting around saying, "It's no big deal, it's OK, it just happens, and there's nothing we can do about it?" No, we'd be educating people about how to avoid catching it, we'd be doing tons of research about it, and we'd have public service announcements about it on TV and on billboards - who knows we might even have a telethon over Labor Day weekend to raise funds to help prevent it.

I know that statistics can be boring, but let me give you a few more shockers:

- only about 2% of high school sweethearts who marry end up having a 50-year marriage - that's only 2 couples out of 100 couples - not very good odds

- only 6% of all people who get married end up having a 50-year marriage - that's only 6 out of 100 couples

So why doesn't our society take more action and do whatever it can to help minimize divorce? I'm not sure, but let me take a few guesses:

Could it be that many of us know couples who used the "Dating without God" approach to dating and so far, they have a happy marriage?

Could it be that some of us know people (maybe even ourselves) who are currently using the "Dating without God" approach to dating and so far, everything has turned out fine?

Could it be that many of us believe that the "Dating without God" approach to dating is the only approach?

Could it be that many of us don't realize there's a significant amount of preparation work that needs to be done prior to dating in order to minimize the possibility of divorce?

Could it be that we don't really want anybody giving us advice about our love life and therefore we feel very uncomfortable giving anyone else advice about their love life?

Could it be that some of us have the "Divorce won't happen to me" attitude? I confess that I used to have that attitude . . . until it happened to me. (I'll share my sad story later in the book.)

Could it be that we don't know how many people's lives are affected by divorce? The Census Bureau says that the number of divorced people has mushroomed from about 4 million in 1970 to almost 20 million in the year 2000.

Shockingly, 50% of all children will live with only one of their parents during their childhood and this missing parent is usually the dad . . . 50% of all children, oh my . . . and we wonder why the world is such a mess. As a school counselor in inner-city schools, I've seen the negative effects that having only one parent can have upon a child. They're missing a role model that they desperately need and their behavior tends to spin out of control more easily than children with two parents.

Could it be that we don't really understand the effects of divorce?

Of course, there are the initial effects of divorce such as incredible stress, pain, shock, confusion, anger, grief, and uncertainty. But studies show that divorce also has long lasting negative effects in many cases - for example:

Depression - Children of divorced parents are seven times more likely to suffer from depression in adult life than people of similar age and background whose parents have not divorced. The loss of a parent through divorce is more likely to cause depression than loss through death

High school dropouts - Teens whose parents are divorced are more likely to drop out of high school that those who have married parents (and the majority of people in prison are high school dropouts)

Drug use - about 70% of children/adolescents in drug rehabilitation hospitals are from single parent families

Suicide - about 60% of suicides are individuals from single parent families

Teenage pregnancies - about 70% of teenage pregnancies are adolescents from single parent homes

Living together and early marriage - Teens whose parents get divorced are more likely to live together, are more likely to marry as teens, and are more likely to marry someone whose parents are also divorced

Future divorce - If a child's parents get divorced, statistics say that it's twice as likely that their marriage will also end in divorce

Could it be that the media and our popular culture have succeeded in convincing many of us that "divorce is no big deal", it's "OK", it "just happens", and "there's not much we can do about it?"

I mean after all; in the media we constantly hear about celebrities getting divorced on a regular basis. It's almost like husbands and wives are disposable like facial tissue. A celebrity was recently married for 72 days. It's no wonder that so many people think that divorce is no big deal - sadly they think, "If I'm not happy with my husband or wife, if they don't treat me right, if I don't get what I want out of my marriage - I'll just get a divorce." When I hear someone say something like this, and I hear it on a regular basis from my students, it makes me think that many people really don't understand the amount of pain and heartbreak that divorce causes. It makes me think that they don't understand that divorce throws millions of women and their children into poverty. It makes me think that they don't understand the number one dream of many children is that their parents will get back together someday.

The truth is that divorce is similar to death except that divorce is the death of a relationship. Don't you think that it's unusual that many people think divorce isn't a big deal - but almost everyone thinks that death is a big deal? Over the years I've come to the conclusion that most of the people who think that divorce is "no big deal" haven't been through a divorce and they haven't seen the tears of children whose parents are getting divorced or who have divorced. Unfortunately, I've experienced the heartbreak of divorce firsthand and through my students - I've felt the pain and cried the tears of divorce and I've seen their pain and their tears - and I wouldn't wish it on anyone.

And please don't listen to the baloney that you may hear in the media about a "good divorce" - all divorces have negative effects upon people and their families. Tearing a family apart always does some damage.

Not only is divorce a big deal, the truth is that divorce isn't "OK", it doesn't "just happen", and there's much that we can do about it. But please don't take my word for it. Let's look at God's word.

If God thought that divorce was "OK", why would He say in Malachi Chapter 2:16 "I hate divorce?" That's pretty strong language - He didn't say it's not a good thing, He didn't say He prefers we didn't do it - He said that He *hates* it. 1 Corinthians 10 and 11 says that "a wife must not separate from her husband and a husband must not divorce his wife." It's clear from these verses that God doesn't think that divorce is "OK." Isn't it amazing that we as a society don't put more effort into minimizing something that God says that He hates?

What does God have to say about the opinion of many people who think divorce is something that "just happens"? Jesus himself shed light upon why people divorce when he says in Matthew 19:8 that "Moses permitted you to divorce your wives because your hearts were hard. But it was not this way from the beginning." He seems to be saying that divorce happens because of the hardness of one's heart - in other words selfishness and stubbornness. When a person is selfish and stubborn, isn't their heart hardened to others - even to their husband or wife? So, it seems that God is telling us that divorce isn't something that "just happens", it's something that's caused by selfish and stubborn thoughts, words, and actions.

And finally, let's look at "there's nothing we can do about it." This simply isn't true. This argument flies in the face of everything we know about God. Mark 10:27 tells us plainly that "all things are possible with God." So that means with God's help we can achieve the goal of minimizing divorce in our society.

So how do we get God's help? - we turn to Him in faith and we live our lives for Him. You may think that living your life for God is going to be dull and boring - but it's not true as you'll see in Chapter 5. Jesus himself describes a life lived for Him in John 10:10, "I came that they (us) may have life, and may have it abundantly." An abundant life is the most exciting, joyous, and fulfilling life possible.

I hope that you'll use the information in this chapter to motivate yourself to do whatever you can to avoid divorce.

Reflection: What negative effect has divorce had upon your immediate family, your extended family, or upon families that you know?

18

4

. . . the power of peers

"Only the power of God can overcome the power of peers"

So, who do you think has a big influence on the behavior of many teens? You guessed it - peers. Many teens are influenced by their peers to participate in behaviors that are contrary to the word of God in order to "fit in." Unfortunately, these behaviors often have lifelong negative consequences.

Since peers influence the behavior of many teens so much, I think I'm safe saying that peers influence the behavior of many teens more than God - our heavenly Father and Ruler of the universe. Do you think that brings a tear to His eye? If you don't agree that peers are more of an influence than God on the behavior of many teens - ask yourself when the last time you heard a teen say something like, "I'm not going to (you fill in the blank) because God doesn't want me to" or "Even though I don't feel like it, I'm going to (you fill in the blank) because I think it's something that God wants me to do." I'm presuming that you haven't heard statements like these very much.

Let's try to understand why peers have more influence and are more important to many teens than God. Could it be that we see and talk to peers every day - and God is someone who we can't see and possibly someone who we don't know how to talk with comfortably every day in prayer?* Could it be that we put more effort into developing our relationships with peers compared to the time we spend developing our relationship with God? Could it be that peers give us feedback (positive and negative) every day? Could it be that peers are so powerful because we think that we need their approval and acceptance in order to feel good about ourselves and we tremendously fear their rejection? Could all of these things be reasons why many teens have a closer relationship with their peers than they do with God? (This isn't the way God wants it to be - it's clear that God wants our relationship with Him to be our closet relationship - why else would Christ say in Matthew, chapter 22, verse 37 that the greatest commandment is to "love the Lord your God with all your heart and with all your soul and with all your mind . . ."?)

Speaking of rejection from peers, I really understand why so many teens fear it and desperately want to "fit in" because I used to feel the same way. Here's an example from my life: I ended up going to a new high school for my senior year because we moved. I didn't know anyone, they didn't know me, and my #1 concern was whether or not people would like me. I was so paranoid and so concerned about people not liking me that I hardly said a word to anyone during the first two months of the school year. I was afraid that if I opened my mouth my peers wouldn't like me (thankfully as the year wore on, I started to talk more and I made a few real friends).

What I didn't realize at the time was that I basically was allowing peers to control my life. Are you or other teens you know making the same mistake? A key turning point in the life of a Christian is when they decide to allow God to be in control of their lives on a daily basis instead of peers or themselves. Caution: After you make this decision to allow God to be in control, don't expect an overnight change in regard to being overly concerned about whether or not your peers like you - it's a gradual process in which God strengthens you and changes you into the person that He wants you to be. You'll know that you're making progress when you notice you're not so concerned about pleasing your peers as you used to be - especially peers who aren't Christians.

Over time you'll reach the point where you'll try to do whatever you think God wants you to do in a particular situation - regardless of what anyone else says, does, or thinks. Here's a suggestion for handling peer rejection: If a peer puts you down because you did what you thought God wanted you to do in a situation, don't worry or make yourself angry about it because that peer isn't your real friend anyway. Instead, make every effort to make some real Christian friends by being a real friend. It's well worth the effort (please see Chapter 6).

So, what do peers have to do with teen dating? Unfortunately, many teens are under extreme pressure from their peers to date before they're spiritually and emotionally ready. This peer pressure is both conscious and unconscious. Consciously, this pressure can take the form of teasing, putting you down because you don't have a boyfriend or girlfriend by saying things like, "anybody who's somebody has a boyfriend or girlfriend", etc. Unconsciously, when a teen sees other teens with a boyfriend or a girlfriend, the natural tendency is to feel a bit inferior and to develop a desire to have a boyfriend or girlfriend also in order to "fit in" and feel good about themselves. (Chapter 7 will talk about the only lasting way for humans to feel good about themselves.)

It may be hard to understand and believe, but when you allow God to be in control of your life on a daily basis, you'll have the best possible life here on earth. You can rely on His power to help you overcome the power of your peers. You may be saying to yourself, "If I put God in control of my life, I won't have any fun!" As you'll see in the next chapter, contrary to popular belief, the Christian lifestyle is the most exciting of all.

*A great short book about prayer is listed on p. 117.

Reflection: How do peers influence your behavior on a daily basis? Positively? Negatively? Do you behave differently when you're around non-Christian peers compared to when you're around Christian peers? If so, why?

"If a large number of people are doing something (for example, speeding in their car, using alcohol or other drugs, dating before they're ready, living together before marriage, etc.) - it's often a sign that it's a bad choice."

5

. . . the Christian lifestyle being the most exciting of all

"Running the race of life with other Christians on the road to heaven is the best place to be. The excitement of living your life for Christ pales in comparison to living your life for yourself."

I used to think that living a Christian lifestyle was kind of boring (you know - being good, prayer, church, etc.) and that it didn't really help to make people happy. I was wrong. Research studies show that people who are living their lives for Christ are happier than those who aren't. I now think it's the most exciting lifestyle of all. There's something very special about:

- living your life for the Creator and Ruler of the entire universe

- being able to confess your sins in prayer and have them forgiven instantly

- being able to put your head on the pillow each night knowing that you're in His loving embrace and that He loves you more than you can imagine

- God helping you to be loving, happy, peaceful, patient, kind, good, faithful, gentle, and self-controlled (see Galatians, chapter 5, verses 22-23)

- having a Christian husband or wife who loves the Lord (if you get married to a person who loves the Lord)

- fellowship with Christian friends - friends who will help, support, and encourage you in times of trouble and who will celebrate with you in times of joy

- knowing that Christ is always with you throughout the ups and downs of life. (Christ never said that our life on earth was going to be easy. Since I've put my faith and trust in Him, I've known that He will help me through this life here on earth no matter how bad things get. And after my earthly life is over, He will keep His promise and I'll live with Him forever. It may sound corny, but I'm getting goose bumps just writing this. Please see Matthew, chapter 28, verse 20.)

I hope that telling the following true story will help you to get a little taste of why the Christian lifestyle is the most exciting on earth: When we lived in a small town in Virginia, our pastor accepted a new position at a large church in Chicago. The church decided to give him a grand sendoff party - and grand it was. In the banquet room of Ernie's restaurant, one group after another from the church performed a humorous skit or song honoring the pastor. We almost couldn't stop laughing. At one point during the evening, the pastor stood on his chair waving his napkin in a big circle above his head with the music blaring in order to pump up the crowd.

A song by the senior citizens was the high point of the evening. The pastor rode a big motorcycle for fun, so six senior citizen ladies dressed up in full-length leather motorcycle outfits and sang on stage the old song "The Leader of the Pack." The laughter was almost deafening. I noticed that the restaurant employees standing off to the side were wide-eyed and amazed about what was going on. Here was a church group, without any alcohol, almost raising the roof off the place and having a great time. That night our church demonstrated in a small way that the Christian lifestyle is the most exciting on earth.

6

. . . our need for Christian friends

"Making the effort required to make and keep real Christian friends is very important - they'll add much joy to your life - find them and they'll be a blessing to you"

You may be asking yourself, "Why are Christian friends so important?" The reason is that God does not want us to go through our life here on earth alone. You need to find a group of Christian friends to be a part of at your church, school, or both. You need to be part of a group with teens who are interested in learning how to live their lives for Christ.

Christian friends will talk with you, encourage you, and help you through the downs of life. They'll celebrate with you during the ups of life, help you to have a closer relationship with Jesus Christ, help you to stay focused on living your life daily for Christ, help you resist peer pressure, give you wise counsel when needed (in other words, tell you what you need to hear even when you don't want to hear it) and hold you accountable for your actions. They'll truly be your friends forever.

A parent recently told me that their teen wants to "fit in" with her peers. Unfortunately, as I mentioned earlier in the book, this desire to "fit in" and "be accepted" by peers often causes teens to make bad choices - choices that take them away from their long-term goals. Please do whatever it takes to find a group of Christian friends with whom you can "fit in." Your best bet is to find a church youth group that has an adult leader who's a strong Christian and participate in the group on a regular basis. It's not easy trying to live your life on earth in a way that's pleasing to God. We need help from our Christian friends and from God Himself.

Just a word of warning about spending too much time with friends who aren't Christians - you tend to become more like the people you hang with, so if you spend a lot of time with people who don't think having a personal relationship with Jesus Christ is important, over time your relationship with Him may become less important to you.

Speaking of non-Christian friends, here's the true story about the first time I ever asked someone out on a date. I was a junior in high school, but I was only fifteen because I started school a year early. I had my eye on a beautiful hot blonde that was a junior varsity cheerleader. (The danger of being too concerned with beauty on the outside is covered in Chapter 14.) I just missed the deadline for fall Driver's Education class so I wasn't going to be able to drive until the spring semester. I wanted to ask this girl out on a date, but I didn't want to have my Dad drive us and pick us up - I would have been too embarrassed.

I told my "friend" Justin (name changed to protect the guilty) about my desire to ask her out on a date. He told me, "I'll drive you if you get a date, but you don't have the guts to ask her." Well, he was wrong. I practiced my asking for a date speech at least 50 times. I planned when and where in the school I would ask her for a date. I thought I had it planned perfectly because I was going to ask her to go to an away basketball game - games at which junior varsity cheerleaders didn't cheer. She didn't know me from Adam, but for some reason - I didn't think that was going to be a problem.

My heart was pounding, my mouth was dry, and the time had come. I walked up along side her in the hall near the end of the school day, turned to her and blurted out - "Hi, my name is Jim, I was wondering if you would consider going with me to the next away basketball game?" She said, "I can't because I have to cheer." Awkwardly, I said, "Oh, I thought you didn't cheer at away games." She said kindly, "It's the only away game

that we're going to cheer at this year - maybe some other time."
I didn't know what to say so I just said, "Thanks." My knees
were shaking as I walked away. It took me about an hour to
completely calm down. That night I told Justin that I had asked
her for a date. His reaction was "What! - I never thought you'd
do it!" I told him that I planned to ask her out again. He said,
"Well if you do - I'm not driving you." That's when I knew he
wasn't a real friend - he didn't keep his word.

I was so shy and embarrassed that even though I saw her in the
hall periodically I never said another word to her. She probably
thought that I was some kind of a jerk. Looking back at it now,
it was probably a blessing that I didn't date her because I was
nowhere near spiritually and emotionally ready to start dating.

A real friend:

- allows you to be yourself, really listens to you, doesn't
  share what's been said

- can be trusted, supports and helps you, treats you with
  respect, sticks with you when other people abandon you

- keeps their word

- encourages you to make a good choice - even when
  others are encouraging you to make a bad choice

- tells you what you need to hear even when you don't
  want to hear it

- helps you to calm yourself down after you've made
  yourself angry

27

- comes and talks with you as soon as possible when there is a problem in the friendship

- is willing to forgive you when you mess up

- understands that friendships change over time and can accept those changes after talking it out

(Please read 1 Samuel, chapter 18, verse 1 through chapter 20, verse 42. It will give you a good idea about what Christian friendship is supposed to be like.)

Reflection: What can you do to have more Christian friends and/or strengthen your existing Christian friendships?

"A person's choice of friends is really important. Strong real friends lift you up. Weak fake friends pull you down."

"Friendships multiply joys and divide griefs."
- Henry George Bohn

"He's my friend that speaks well of me behind my back."
- Thomas Fuller

7

. . . why dating is so important to teens

"Sad but true - humans will do almost anything to feel good about themselves"

Have you noticed that teens try to feel good about themselves in positive and negative ways? For example: by being good at a sport, by winning a game, by playing an instrument well, by being a good person, by having lots of friends, by being an excellent student, by doing great work at a part-time job, by being a fan of a winning team, by buying as much stuff as possible, by using alcohol and other drugs, by putting down other people, by being tough and mean, by winning a fight with someone else, by gambling - the list goes on and on.

If you polled teens about the reasons why they want to date you might get responses like: "I really like him", "I really like her", "he's really exciting", "she's hot", "he's cute", "most of my friends are dating", "I want to have fun", among others.

My guess is that many teens won't mention one of the main reasons if you ask them. I would like to suggest that one of the main reasons teens want to date is that they want to feel good about themselves and/or they want to feel loved. After all it's only human nature - we want to have someone who really cares about us, we want to feel important, we want to be respected by our peers, and we want to feel attractive to the opposite sex. Being in a dating relationship usually helps us to feel good about ourselves. May I suggest that our feeling good about ourselves and feeling loved isn't supposed to come from being in a dating relationship and it's not supposed to come from any of the other things we do that were mentioned at the beginning of this chapter. Our unshakable feeling good about ourselves is supposed to come from having a close personal relationship with Jesus Christ. If we have trusted in Christ alone as our Savior, we understand that because of this choice we are now a child of God forever, that He loves us unconditionally, and that one day we will live with Him for eternity. Wow, aren't these great reasons to feel good about yourself! *Becoming a Christian and living a Christian life is the only lasting way for a person to feel good about himself or herself.*

<u>Reflection:</u> How important is dating to you and why?

8

. . . our culture teaching us that early dating is OK

"I really need a boyfriend. Almost all of my friends have one."

A few years back my six-year-old told me proudly, "I have eight girlfriends." It was an innocent comment that sheds light on what our culture teaches us about dating. It teaches us that having a girlfriend or boyfriend before we're spiritually and emotionally ready is "normal", "acceptable", "a good thing", or "cute." Obviously, we learn it at an early age. You've probably heard a parent or a grandparent proudly say with a smile something like, "Kristen is thirteen and she already has a boyfriend" or "Evan is fifteen, he's dating, in fact he's had three girlfriends already."

Unfortunately, our culture doesn't emphasize the importance of teens going on the journey of preparing themselves for dating and the result is that most teens start to date before they're ready using the "Dating without God" approach. These teens often get into an unhealthy pattern of becoming emotionally attached quickly to another person and then eventually tearing that attachment apart (breaking up) when they don't "feel like" being attached anymore. This breakup often causes one or both people to go through the anguish of having their heart broken. Regretfully, many teens don't learn from their mistakes and soon after their breakup they start the pattern all over again with someone else. They don't realize that being in this pattern damages their emotions.

People who have developed this pattern of behavior during their teenage years often continue it by eventually finding "the person of their dreams", getting engaged, getting married, and eventually when they don't "feel like" being married - getting divorced. Breaking the close emotional attachment of marriage is much, much easier than it otherwise would be. Why? It's because they've broken an emotional attachment so many times before. Does that make sense? Unfortunately, even after divorce a large number of people still don't learn from their mistakes and they repeat the same pattern again because they don't even know that they're in a pattern. Unfortunately, many celebrities have this problem.

Hopefully this book will help you to avoid getting into this unhealthy pattern or will help you to get out of it if you're already in it (by using "Dating with God" approach to dating as explained in Chapter 16).

Reflection: Do you think that a person should be dating before they're a freshman in high school? Why or why not?

9

. . . dating at an early age usually is a big mistake

"Raging teenage hormones combined with dating at an early age is like a train going around a curve at ninety miles an hour with two loose wheels"

When a teen starts to date before they're spiritually and emotionally ready, the more likely they'll . . .

. . . not do their best in school (because they spend too much time interacting with their boyfriend or girlfriend and not enough time on homework and studying)

. . . have sex before marriage

. . . contract one or more sexually transmitted diseases

. . . become a parent without being married

. . . marry before they're ready

. . . marry someone who's not ready to be married

. . . marry someone that God doesn't want them to marry

. . . have an unhappy unfulfilling marriage

. . . be divorced in their lifetime

Some teens have told me that they don't think that it's really necessary to prepare themselves for dating - they just want things to happen "naturally" and "fall in love." Sadly, many of these teens end up messing up their lives because of their bad dating choices and because they don't know the difference between the feeling of being "in love" and true love. (Please see Chapter 17 for an explanation of the difference.)

Reflection: Has early dating had a negative effect upon you or upon someone you know?

"Dating, if done right, can possibly lead to the most wonderful experience that you'll ever have here on earth - a beautiful lifelong loving Christian marriage."

10

. . . how to become a keeper - the type of person that God wants you to date

"Build your house (your life) upon the solid rock of Jesus Christ - He will give you joy, He will be with you always, and He will help you through the storms of life"

The first step in the "Dating with God" approach to dating is to become a keeper. You've probably heard the expression "He's a keeper" or "She's a keeper", which means that a person has valuable characteristics that a person would want in a boyfriend or girlfriend, husband or wife.

From a Christian perspective, may I suggest that a keeper is a strong Christian, someone who *keeps*:

- their Christian faith strong through daily prayer, and regular Bible study/church attendance

- trusting in Christ alone for their salvation and for their daily needs

- trusting God when the storms of life hit (problems, tragedies, etc.)

- God in mind when making any important decision (In other words, they seek God's will for their lives.)

- their spending under control

- trying to obey the two greatest commandments, "love the Lord your God with all your heart and with all your

35

soul and with all your mind and with all your strength" and "love your neighbor as yourself." (Mark, chapter 12, verses 28-31)

- trying to grow throughout their life (spiritually, personally, emotionally, relationally, and intellectually)

- trying to display the fruits of the Holy Spirit - love, joy, peace, patience, kindness, goodness, faithfulness, gentleness, and self-control

- a group of Christian friends

- trying to control their tongue

- a positive attitude

- themselves sexually pure from this day forward*

- in mind how much God loves them regardless of what they've done

- forgiving others

If a keeper decides to get married, they're someone who *keeps*:

- trying to meet the needs of their husband or wife

- trying to communicate their needs to their husband or wife in a positive manner

- trying to resolve conflicts with their husband or wife in a calm constructive manner

- trying to treat their husband or wife with a high level of concern and respect in both words and actions -

36

regardless of what they receive in return from their husband or wife

- making the effort required to keep the feeling of being "in love" at a high level (more about this later)

- their lifelong commitment to their husband or wife

Unfortunately, instead of taking the time necessary to become a keeper, millions of teens are making the mistake of spending too much of their valuable time trying to develop a relationship with a member of the opposite sex (please keep in mind that just because millions are making this mistake - it doesn't mean that you should just go along with the crowd).

The media and our popular culture constantly emphasize how important these relationships are. The fact is that a human relationship should never ever be your most important relationship - your most important relationship should be the one with Jesus Christ. It's absolutely essential to become a keeper by developing a strong personal relationship with your Savior before you even think about developing a relationship with a boyfriend or girlfriend.

You may be asking yourself, "How in the world do I go about developing a strong personal relationship with Jesus Christ?" First of all, if you're not already, you need to become a Christian as is explained starting on p. 125.

The next thing you need to do is to make a commitment to the goal of becoming the type of person that God wants you to date - not a halfhearted commitment, but an "I'm going to do whatever it takes, nothing is going to stop me" commitment.**

In order to accomplish this goal, you're going to have to take the time and put in the effort that's needed in order to achieve it. A big part of the motivation to accomplish this goal has to come from within yourself. You also need to realize that unfortunately you can't become the type of person that God wants you to date on your own. You need His help in order to achieve this goal. A good way to receive His help is to ask for it in daily prayer, maybe a prayer as simple as "help me Father today to become more like the person you want me to be."

Next, you need to set aside time every day to develop your relationship with Him. I can almost hear you saying, "I haven't got time for that - I've got too many things that I have to get done, too many things that I want to do." It's easy to let extracurricular activities, friends, and electronics (cell phone, computer, TV, whatever the latest electronic gadget is) squeeze out your daily time with God. A lesson that I've learned from school and work is that I'm most effective when I make it a point to always work first on the highest priority thing that I need to do. I know it's going to be tough, but you need to make spending time developing your relationship with Jesus Christ your highest priority.

Here are some reasons why:

- Because Jesus said that one of the greatest commandments is to "love the Lord your God with all your heart and with all your soul and with all your mind and with all your strength . . ." (if we love God, we're supposed to obey Him)

- Because having a close relationship with Jesus Christ will help you to make good decisions in life as well as help you to make it through the tough times in life (Hebrews, chapter 13, verse 5 says that the Lord has promised that He will never leave or abandon us)

- Because you have a built-in teacher - when you become a Christian the Holy Spirit (God) comes into your heart. Jesus says in John, chapter 14, verse 26 that the Holy Spirit will teach you all things as well as remind you of what He said while He was on earth. In other words, the Holy Spirit teaches us how to live our lives in a way that's pleasing to God. The Holy Spirit also teaches us how to have the fruits of the Spirit.

- Because having a close relationship with Jesus Christ will help you to have the best possible life here on earth and it will prepare you to live forever with Him in heaven

Here are more suggestions of how to go about developing your relationship with Him: 1. Get yourself a good Bible that's written for teens. Read it every other day at the least - start out in John and move to other books that talk about daily living and love - such as Proverbs, 1 Corinthians, etc. 3. Spend time in prayer daily including praising God; thanking Him for all of your blessings; confessing your sins of thought, word, and deed; asking God to forgive your sins; asking Him to help you forgive other people; asking God for wisdom to make good decisions that are pleasing to Him; asking God for strength to live your life each day the way he wants you to; sharing things with Him that are bothering or worrying you; and praying for other people.

It's also helpful to use some of your prayer time to be silent and listen to God. And finally, if you're not already, start listening to your choice of Christian music instead of music about relationships between men and women - there's some great Christian music out there and it can help you to have a closer relationship with Jesus Christ.

Here's a list of suggested priorities in life: #1 - daily time in prayer, #2 - eating a balanced diet and sleeping between nine and ten hours per night***, #3 - time reading the Bible or devotionals (possibly every other day), #4 - time with your family, #5 - schoolwork, homework, and studying #6 - time with Christian friends (please see Chapter 6), #7 - involvement with your church and other Christian organizations, #8 - exercise (at least three times a week if approved by your doctor), #9 - reading biblically sound books written from a Christian perspective such as those recommended in the Appendix, #10 - everything else. Sure, you're going to have to carefully budget your time, but with God's help - you can do it!

Doesn't it make sense to spend a large amount of time in your teenage years building the foundation of your life on the rock, Jesus Christ, by developing a close relationship with Him - instead of wasting too much of your time trying to develop a human relationship (dating) which hardly ever results in a lifelong loving Christian marriage? Please see Matthew, chapter 7, verses 24-27.

You'll know that you're making progress toward your goal of becoming the type of person that God wants you to date when you have more and more of the characteristics of a keeper as described in Chapter 12.

*We have an awesome God who loves us more than we can imagine. He will forgive us for whatever we've done if we come to Him in faith (remember that Christians aren't perfect, just forgiven).

**Please see pp. 116 -117 for information about a book that will help you grow spiritually.

***According to doctors, teens need more sleep than adults because they're still developing.

11

. . . why it's crucial to become a keeper before dating

"A person who becomes a keeper before dating is more likely to have a lifelong loving Christian marriage"

The Bible makes it very clear in 2 Corinthians, chapter 6, verse 14 that we're not to be yoked (attached) with unbelievers. So, in other words, God doesn't want a Christian to marry someone who's not a Christian. So how do you do your best to prevent that from happening? Here are two suggestions:

- Do whatever it takes to become a keeper before you start dating - discussed in the last chapter and this chapter

- Do whatever it takes to only date another keeper - discussed in the next chapter

You need to understand that if you've decided to trust in Christ alone as your Savior, you're now a child of God and He loves you dearly. You're a treasure to Him and He only wants the best for you. He wants you to have the best possible life here on earth and when He decides that your physical body is going to die, He will take you to heaven to live with Him forever (what a wonderful thought, think about it).

As you grow in your relationship with Jesus Christ, you'll eventually come to the point where you'll be fully devoted to Him . . . you'll feel strongly that your relationship with Him is at the center of your life, you'll want to spend time with Him every day to grow that relationship, you'll love Him dearly, and

41

you'll have decided to put Him in control of your life instead of yourself. This process of becoming a keeper takes time . . . possibly several years. After all, how can you tell if you're really fully devoted to Christ unless that devotion has stood the test of time during the ups and downs of life?

So, please don't even think about dating until you're sure that you're a keeper. If you're a female and someone asks you out, tell them, "Sorry, but I have decided not to date at this time." You'll probably be ridiculed by others, but shouldn't you be more concerned with pleasing God than you are with pleasing humans? If you're a male, please forget about asking someone out until you're a keeper. Ask God in prayer to give you strength to stand up against the peer pressure to date. (I realize that peer pressure seems overwhelming, but even more overwhelming is the power of God if you tap into it through daily prayer - ask Him for strength. Christian friends can also help you to be strong - please see Chapter 6.)

If you're a keeper and someday marry a keeper it means that you've built your house (your marriage) on a foundation of rock (Jesus Christ). That means that when the storms of life come - in the form of problems, conflict, and possibly even tragedy - your marriage will be much more likely to survive the storm. Another way to think about it is that when the going gets tough, strong Christian faith is the glue that helps to hold couples together. Ecclesiastes, chapter 4, verse 12 says, "A rope made from three strands of cord is hard to break." The three strands are God, man, and woman.

12

. . . why it's important to only date a keeper
and how to recognize one

"Be careful because wolves often disguise themselves in sheep's clothing"

Not many people are interested in holding a stick of dynamite that's just been lit. But that's exactly what you'll be doing if you decide to date someone who's not a keeper. The reason is that it's just too easy to become emotionally attached to someone who's a non-Christian or a weak Christian. No matter how nice, how cute, how beautiful, how handsome, how wonderful, or how much money they have - please don't do it.

I know it sounds black and white, you might even be saying to yourself, "what could one date hurt?", but I need to warn you about the possible consequences. You need to realize that you're setting yourself up to become emotionally attached to someone who God doesn't want you to marry. You're setting yourself up for misery and heartbreak. Unfortunately, I know - I made this mistake.

Here's my painful story: I met a young lady at a fraternity (one with a Christian emphasis) party during my senior year of college. She was beautiful on the outside (the dangers of which are described in Chapter 14). We talked for about two hours, we seemed to have some things in common, and I ended up walking her back to her dorm. We had many dates, she said that she was a Christian, and we went to church together just about every week while we were dating. We dated for about two years before we made the bad choice to get married.

After we got married it seemed like she was a completely different person than she was while we were dating. It was quite a shock to me because I didn't have any experience dealing with an angry unhappy person. Can you imagine having things like a pot being thrown at you in a fit of rage, ducking, and having it crash into the wall behind you? Looking back at it, I now realize that I didn't do a good enough job of using dating to find out what she was really like (as discussed in Chapter 16).

After nine years of marriage, she told me that she wanted to do "her own thing" and she moved out. On the day of the divorce hearing, just over ten years from when we were married, the judge asked her why she was seeking a divorce. She didn't have a reason. It wasn't until years later that I realized the two big mistakes that I had made - I dated when I was not yet a keeper and I dated a person who was not a keeper.

The good news is that with God's help I didn't make the same mistakes twice. He has blessed me with a wonderful wife who's a keeper and two precious sons.

Here's a list of characteristics that may help you to recognize a keeper (please be aware that some people who behave like a keeper aren't really a keeper - in other words, they're putting on an act):

1. They try to live their life for Christ on a daily basis

2. They freely tell others that they're a Christian and share the difference that Jesus Christ has made in their life

3. They've been a Christian and have been living a Christian lifestyle for several years (the longer the better)

4. They continuously seek God's will for their life - in other words, they ask for God's guidance and help in every important decision

5. The most important relationship in their life is their relationship with Jesus Christ

6. They have a close relationship with Him

7. They desire to grow (deepen) their relationship with Him and they're taking action to do so (please see #8-11)

8. They spend time in daily prayer

9. They read the Bible on a regular basis

10. They read biblically sound books written from a Christian perspective

11. They develop friendships with other Christians

12. They recognize and accept God's authority over them - their behavior reflects this fact

13. They try their best to obey God's word

14. They display the fruits of the Holy Spirit

15. They treat everyone with kindness and respect - even people who are disrespected by others

16. They have empathy and compassion for others

17. They're a giving person, not a selfish person

18. They admit their mistakes and take responsibility for their actions

19. They ask for forgiveness as needed and they willingly forgive other people

20. They feel good about themselves based upon their position as a child of God

21. They belong to a church that's helping them to grow spiritually. They give volunteer service to the church in some capacity. They donate money to the church consistently as part of their personal budget.

Reflection: What's your plan of action for becoming (if you're not already) and remaining a keeper?

"A good name is more desired than great wealth."
- Proverbs

13

. . . the importance of emotional and financial maturity

"Dating a person without emotional and/or financial maturity can lead to disaster"

In the last three chapters I talked about the importance of spiritual maturity - becoming a keeper and then only dating another keeper. Before you date, please also consider emotional and financial maturity.

Unfortunately, many people aren't emotionally mature enough to start dating (they, of course, will tell you otherwise). Some people are emotionally needy - they need to be in a relationship with someone in order to feel good about themselves. These people often are dependent and they don't know how to take care of themselves. In other words, they need to have someone take care of them. You need to be aware of the dangers of dating this type of person. They become emotionally attached very quickly and demand a lot of attention - they tend to suffocate you with their needs. Many people who aren't emotionally mature are selfish. You don't want to date and marry a selfish person. Selfishness is discussed in more detail in Chapter 24.

You'll see in Chapter 25 that problems controlling money is one of the ten main causes of divorce. Many people have never been taught by their parents how to control money. They earn or are given money, but it slips through their fingers very quickly without much to show for it. It's very important that at least one marriage partner has the ability to earn what's needed to support the family and that both people know how to spend money wisely. Over the years I have known many couples whose marriage was damaged because of careless spending and having too much credit card debt. Some of these couples ended up getting divorced because one or both of them was unable or unwilling to control their spending. Please take the time to read at least one good book about how to control your money using a budget that includes saving for the future.*

In an ideal world, it would be great if people would enter into a marriage relationship only if they're keepers and have several years of full-time work experience (experience after they've completed their education). This is when it's more likely that people will have the emotional and financial maturity needed to be married. It's almost like concrete - when you first graduate from high school, college, or technical school and start a full-time job, the concrete for the foundation of your building (your life) has just been poured. Your identity, who you are as a person, is still in the process of being formed. It takes a few years for the concrete to fully harden, to be at its full strength. It's not good to join two buildings together (marriage) when one or both of the buildings have weak concrete. The possibility of collapse (divorce) of the relationship is much higher.

*Please see p. 118 for information about a book that can help you learn how to control your money. A suggestion I've heard for engaged couples is that they write down exactly what they spend during one month. Then, at the end of the month, they sit down and go over the list - asking each other questions about why every expenditure was made. Following this suggestion will help the couple to see whether or not they are able to spend money wisely. My wife and I have an agreement that we don't spend more than sixty dollars on anything that's not in the budget without first talking about it. A good credit card rule is to use them only for emergency expenditures.

14

. . . how being too concerned with beauty on the outside can cause you to fall into a trap

"Don't let beauty on the outside make you blind to ugliness on the inside"

Our society and the media are completely caught up in beauty on the outside. Just look at magazines, TV, and the movies. Men especially are attracted visually. When we get caught up in beauty on the outside, our brains tend to stop working. We don't see or we ignore obvious serious problems because they're "beautiful", "cute", or "good looking." Millions and millions of people have fallen into this trap - including me.

The key thing that we all need to remember is that beauty on the outside eventually fades, but beauty on the inside lasts forever. If you decide one day to get married, God wants you to marry someone who's beautiful on the inside - a person with Godly character who displays the fruits of the Holy Spirit. It's a joy to spend each day with such a person.

<u>Reflection:</u> Have you or someone you know made a dating choice mainly based upon looks? Was it a good choice?

"A person with true beauty has a positive caring personality combined with Godly character."

"Unfortunately, a person who is beautiful or handsome on the outside is sometimes ugly on the inside - because their looks go to their head."

Notes:

15

. . . "The Checklist"

"Guard your heart by being careful about whom you date"

When you're a keeper and you're emotionally as well as financially mature enough to start dating, you should look for a person to date who:

- is a keeper

- has a good sense of humor, can laugh at their own mistakes

- has things in common with you (recreational interests, hobbies, values, lifestyle during childhood, etc.)

- has a compatible personality to yours (Do you both tend to be introverted (shy, not very talkative) or extroverted (outgoing, talkative)? It's true that opposites often attract, but be careful. Statistics show that people with similar personalities are more likely to have a lifelong loving marriage.

- displays the fruits of the Holy Spirit

- has integrity (They're truthful with you and with others. They recognize their weaknesses and admit their mistakes. They try to make a good choice in every situation regardless of how difficult it is, what it costs them, or what other people think.)

- honors their mother and father

- is a hard worker (but not a workaholic)

- thinks that getting a good education is very important and gives their best effort in school

- has a positive, cheerful attitude the vast majority of the time

- is able to control their tongue (please see Chapter 22)

- desires to grow continually in their Christian faith as well as personally and emotionally

- treats all people with respect (even people who are usually disrespected by others)

- has a healthy level of self-esteem (not too high and not too low)

- is a giving person

When you're ready to start dating, avoid dating a person who:

- isn't a keeper

- wants you to take care of them

- doesn't really want to grow up

- doesn't take responsibility for their actions (in other words, they think that almost everything that goes wrong is somebody else's fault)

- is easily angered

- complains about something on a regular basis

- expresses their negative feelings (frustration, anger, etc.) in a destructive manner (yelling, swearing, putting others down, throwing things, etc.)

- wants to control you by telling you what to do and/or by keeping you away from your Christian friends

- you think that you need to change

- is a selfish person

Your reaction to this checklist may have been something like, "Where in the world am I going to find a person like that - someone who almost walks on water?"

Please remember that when you put in the effort required to become the type of person that's described in this checklist, it makes it much more likely that you'll be able to attract the same type of person - and with God's help, "all things are possible."

(Please see p. 105 for a list of 21 tips that can help you attract a keeper.)

Reflection: What's your reaction to the checklist? What makes sense in the checklist and what doesn't?

Question: What do you think are the most important ingredients of a good relationship?

If I had to boil it all down to the four main ingredients that are necessary in order to have a positive healthy dating relationship and possibly a lifelong loving Christian marriage - I'd have to say: #1: both people being a keeper #2: both people having emotional and financial maturity #3: having lots and lots of things in common with each other #4: chemistry. You can find out through dating whether or not both of you are keepers, whether or not both of you are emotionally and financially mature, whether or not you have many things in common (your hobbies and interests, your political viewpoint, your opinion about how children should be raised, your thoughts about how money should be spent, etc.) and whether or not you have good positive chemistry - the feeling that you really "click" with each other. Unfortunately, many people make disastrous dating and marriage choices mainly based upon whether they like someone and looks. Please use dating to be absolutely sure that all four of these main ingredients are there before you even think about the possibility of getting married. It's much easier to build a strong relationship using all of the ingredients than it is to repair an unhappy or broken marriage.

Notes:

16

. . . the "Dating with God" approach to dating and danger signs to watch out for

"Be yourself and use dating to gradually peel away their mask"

If you remember from Chapter 2, I promised to give you specific suggestions for using the "Dating with God" approach. So here goes:

1. Take time to educate yourself about dating and marriage from a Christian perspective by reading some good books - possibly together with some Christian friends (a list of recommended books is included in the Appendix).

2. Please find a way to get to know other people and to discover who's a keeper before you ask anyone out or you agree to go on a date with anyone. My suggestion for doing this is to participate in as many wholesome activities as possible with other people who may be keepers without dating. Sunday School class, church youth group meetings and activities, church committees, church events, coed sports teams, activities of a Christian organization (for example, Young Life, Youth for Christ, Fellowship of Christian Athletes), service projects, mission trips, Bible studies, etc., can all be great opportunities to get to know the type of people that God wants you to date without actually dating. Please keep in mind that some of the people you'll meet are simply masquerading as keepers - take the time necessary to really get to know them.

Here's how I went about getting to know my future wife and discovering that she was a keeper without dating: I met her in a young adult Sunday School class. She and I were just acquaintances for about a year. During this time, I was observing all of the ladies in the class to see how they related to other people. My goal was to get to know the ladies as much as possible without dating (I realize that this is easier for a man to do than it would be for a woman). I tried to participate in the group activities of the class (retreats, football game parties, service projects, etc.) so that I would have a chance to observe their behavior outside of Sunday School class.

I knew that I was looking for a person who displayed the fruits of the Holy Spirit. Pam showed them in the way that she related to everyone. She was upbeat and personable. I never heard her say an unkind word to anyone. She especially impressed me with the amount of time that she spent talking with a mentally disabled lady in the class. While most of the ladies ignored this person or tried to keep their conversations with her short, Pam struck up a conversation with her on a regular basis, asked her questions, and seemed genuinely interested in her as a person. Her kindness to this lady really attracted me to Pam. I started to pray to God about who He wanted me to ask out on a date. Then I specifically asked God if He wanted me to ask Pam out. I asked God this question in prayer for about a month.

I felt that He was leading me to ask her out and so I did one day after Sunday School class. She has been the biggest blessing of my life ever since that day and I'll love her until the day I die. I thank God for her every night in my prayers.

3. Have patience, have perseverance, and talk with God daily in prayer. When you're feeling lonely and discouraged it's hard to be patient, it's hard to persevere, it's hard to keep praying - but with God's help you can do it. God has a wonderful plan for your life - please don't mess it up through impatience, by not sticking to the "Dating with God" approach, and by not staying in close communication with Him. It may be hard to believe, but it's better to be old and lonely than it is to be married to someone that God doesn't want you to be married to.

Presuming that you're a keeper and you're about to go out with a keeper - and you're old enough for group or one-on-one dating (age suggestions are on p. 95) - here are more suggestions for using the "Dating with God" approach:

Do:

- ask God to be the head (in control) of your dating relationship

- participate in a wide variety of wholesome activities and talk about a wide variety of appropriate subjects

- try to find out if you have lots of things in common (having lots of things in common helps to hold a relationship together)

- go to church with him or her

- find out if he or she has a strong set of Christian friends (If he or she's a loner, they may be looking for you to meet all of their needs - this can put a strain on any relationship)

- ask yourself the question: Is his or her focus in life on loving God and loving others or is it on himself or herself? Selfishness is a danger sign (see Chapter 24)

- eventually ask him or her to read this book and the "must read" book, *Fall in Love Stay in Love*, by Dr. Willard F. Harley, Jr. A good idea is to read a chapter or two at a time and then talk about it. Ask each other questions like, "What were the most important points of the chapter to you?", "What in the chapter didn't you agree with?", etc. Share and discuss your *reflections*.

- ask God in prayer on a regular basis if He wants you to continue the dating relationship - seek His direction.

- after prayers asking for wisdom and guidance, break off a relationship with a person to whom you know that God doesn't want you to be married. Do it in a kind but firm way.* Don't be sucked into the trap of going back into the relationship because now you're alone. Remember that Christ is with you always and that He will help you through anything. Ask Him for strength.

Observe:

- his or her words and deeds in all type of situations - does he or she display the fruits of the Holy Spirit consistently?

- if he or she shows respect to all other people - pay special attention to how he or she treats others who are often not well treated by the world (people in low paying jobs, people with disabilities, etc.) Unfortunately, a person who treats others with disrespect will more than likely eventually treat you with disrespect.

- if he or she has compassion toward other people and animals (does he or she have a tender heart?)

- how he or she reacts when something goes wrong and when he or she doesn't get their way or what they want - this will help you to get an idea of what his or her domestic personality is like. I read in a book, I think by the late pastor O. Dean Martin, that we have a social personality and a domestic personality. The social personality is the one that we usually display in public - you know the cheerful and positive one. The domestic personality is the one that we display when we aren't out in public, our guards are down, and we aren't putting on a face - it's more like the real us. It's the personality that you're going to have to live with on a daily basis if you decide to get married. After I was engaged to my first wife, she asked me if I would stay with her mother and her for several weeks while her father was out of town. A few weeks earlier they had an attempted break-in at their house and they didn't want to stay alone while he was away. She was asking me to drive a total of three hours every day to and from work. When I hesitated, she said in not the nicest tone, "Oh, I knew you wouldn't do it!" Unfortunately, I didn't realize it at the time, but she had just revealed some of her domestic personality.

- how he or she treats his or her parents/siblings and other relatives (a lack of love and respect toward his or her family is a danger sign)

- how his or her father and mother relate to each other (Does one dominate the other? - a danger sign, Does one or both of them have a problem controlling their spending?, Do they seem to have a warm loving respectful marriage relationship? - often patterns in the parent's marriage are repeated in the child's marriage)

- if he or she's too concerned with what other people think about him or her - instead of being concerned about what God thinks

- if he or she makes a good choice in situations when making a bad choice could personally benefit him or her - you're looking for a person who will make a good choice (what's pleasing to God) no matter what

- if he or she spends their money wisely

- if he or she takes responsibility for their actions and asks for forgiveness after messing up

Don't:

- put on an act and pretend to be someone you aren't just to make the person you're dating like you (just as you're trying to find out what the person you're dating is really like, the person you're dating wants to get to know the real you - be yourself)

- let the thrill of someone treating you well and making you feel special cause you to ignore obvious serious problems or blind you to the fact that the person you're dating isn't a keeper

- let the fact that the person you're dating has money, or will probably earn a lot of money in the future blind you to their serious problems. Too many people have learned the hard way that the saying, "money doesn't buy happiness" is true.

- ignore the danger of infatuation (the feeling of being "head over heels in love" with someone that you don't really know) - a warning sign of infatuation is that you think about him or her all the time

- become emotionally attached too quickly - guard your heart by taking things nice and slow

- be fooled that the excessive attention of a boyfriend or a girlfriend is true love - excessive attention is often something that people use to control others

- continue in a dating relationship with a boyfriend or girlfriend who has serious problems as discussed in

Chapter 1, tries to control you (for example, tells you what to do or wear), is possessive or jealous, is pressuring you to have sex before marriage, treats you with disrespect verbally or physically*, tries to keep you away from your Christian friends, or with whom the chemistry just isn't there

- pray alone with him or her unless you've already decided to become engaged after going through the careful marriage decision making process described in Chapter 21. (Praying together can cause people who are dating to become emotionally attached too soon.)

- rush into thinking about getting married - statistics show that longer dating relationships are more likely to become lifelong marriage relationships. My suggestion is that you date for at least two years in order to really get to know the other person (wisely use this dating time to talk about almost everything and to carefully observe them in all types of situations in order to find out if they really are a keeper). I also suggest that you wait until you're at least age 24 before you even think about getting married (statistics show that the divorce rate drops significantly if you wait until you're at least 24 or 25 and even more if you wait until 28 - I know that sounds like a long time, but don't you want to maximize the possibly that you'll have a lifelong loving Christian marriage?). Please take the time needed to be absolutely sure that this is the person that God wants you to marry. (Please see Chapter 13 about why early marriages often collapse.)

- isolate yourself from your Christian friends

- spend much alone together (especially if you haven't graduated from high school)

- participate in long make out sessions (Please consider eliminating make out sessions altogether or at least keeping them short - for example 15 minutes - because they can be harmful)

Your reaction to this suggestion may range from "That makes some sense" all the way to "That's absolutely crazy, no one does that." So how can long make out sessions during dating be harmful?

1. They often cause an emotional attachment to develop too quickly in a dating relationship. An emotional attachment can cause a person to ignore serious problems in their significant other and to continue in a dating relationship with a person that God doesn't want them to continue dating. Remember that He tells us to guard our heart and not give it too soon to another person. Please see Proverbs, chapter 4, verse 23.

2. We get addicted to the feelings (caused by chemicals that are released in the brain) that we get when we kiss passionately. This addiction can also cause a person to pay no attention to serious problems and to continue in a dating relationship with a person that God doesn't want them to continue dating. The passions aroused during long make out sessions are designed by God to be expressed only in marriage.

3. If you participate in long make out sessions, over time they tend to gradually take up more and more of the time that you spend together as a couple - they waste important time that you should be using instead to really get to know the other person.

4. People who engage in long make out sessions during dating are much more likely to have premarital sex because they lose control of their passions. Since God tells us to flee from sexual immorality in 1 Corinthians, chapter 6, verse 18, it's clear that He doesn't want us to spend our time before marriage getting

ourselves aroused - not because He wants to spoil our fun, but because He created us and He knows what's best for us.

- touch another person's body anywhere that would not be pleasing to God - save God's gift of sexuality for your husband or wife

- lay down together or turn out the lights - I know this may sound ridiculous and old fashioned, but keeping your feet on the floor and keeping the lights on are good ways to help prevent things from getting out of hand

- drink alcohol - it definitely impairs your God given judgment and often leads to other bad choices

- tell him or her that you love him or her until you fully understand what true love is (please see Chapter 17)

- have sex with him or her before marriage

Some teens think, "What's the big deal about having sex before marriage? - everyone's doing it." First of all, the fact is that everyone isn't doing it. According to a national survey, less than half of all high school students have had sex.

God tells us multiple times in His word that He doesn't want us to have sex before marriage (1 Corinthians chapter 6, verse 13; Matthew chapter 15, verse 19; Ephesians chapter 5, verse 3, etc.).

Secondly, you need to know that having sex before marriage can be harmful to you and to your future. This harm could possibly include:

- not feeling good about having sex before marriage and/or about yourself

- finding out that having sex during dating causes people to become emotionally attached way too quickly

- discovering that having sex makes you want to keep dating someone who you know you shouldn't

- realizing that sex has become the main focus of your dating relationship

- feeling that you need to keep having sex with your boyfriend or girlfriend or else they'll dump you

- not feeling good about choosing to have sex after your boyfriend or girlfriend said "I love you" and then later finding out he or she was lying to you just to get sex or finding out that he or she doesn't even know what true love is

- feeling that you can't get out of a relationship that you know isn't good for you because you're having sex

- finding out too late that dating relationships which have sex as their main focus rarely last

- feeling horrible after being dumped

- becoming an angry person after being dumped

- becoming depressed or possibly even suicidal after being dumped (Please see a qualified pastor or Christian counselor immediately for help if you feel this way.)

- feeling that you can't trust anyone anymore after being dumped

- becoming hesitant about making a lifelong marriage commitment in the future after being dumped

- feeling horrible that you dumped someone else and broke their heart

- getting into the habit of jumping from one sexual relationship to another looking for true love and sadly never finding it

- finding out after you married a person that God didn't want you to marry that having sex before marriage made you ignore serious problems - problems that could destroy your marriage

- contracting a sexually transmitted disease

- getting pregnant and becoming a single parent

- having a child who doesn't have a stable male role model in his or her life (statistics show that teen boys rarely marry their pregnant girlfriends)

- ending up having problems relating sexually to your husband or wife in marriage because of the sex you had with them (and possibly with others) before marriage

- having your husband or wife cheat on you (people who have sex before marriage are much more likely to cheat)

- becoming divorced (statistics show that couples who have sex before marriage are more likely to eventually get divorced than couples who don't have sex before marriage)

My hope is that you'll use this list of suggestions to really get to know the person you're dating. Many divorced people feel that they rushed into marriage and they wish that they would have used dating to get to know what their ex-husband or ex-wife was really like before they decided to get married. It's true that using the "Dating with God" approach isn't easy, but it's much easier than trying to repair an unhappy marriage.

If you've had premarital sex in the past, now is a great time to remain sexually pure until marriage. If you're currently having sex - it's going to be hard, but now is a great time to stop and remain sexually pure until marriage. If you put your faith and trust in God, He will forgive you and He will help you through anything - including the pain of a broken heart if your boyfriend or girlfriend dumps you because you stop having sex with them. It may be difficult to understand, but if your boyfriend or girlfriend dumps you for this reason - they don't have true love for you in their heart as described in Chapter 17 and God doesn't want you to marry them.

If you need help recovering from a broken heart or overcoming the need to be in a sexual relationship before marriage, I urge you to contact a qualified pastor or Christian counselor.

In summary, using the "Dating with God" approach to dating will make it more likely that you'll eventually have lifelong loving Christian marriage.

*If you fear that he or she will have a violent reaction when you break off the dating relationship in a kind manner, ask your parent/guardian for help and/or contact your local Domestic Violence Hotline or the National Hotline at 1-800-799-7233.

17

. . . true love being much more than just the feeling of being "in love"

"What the world needs now is love, true love"

Unfortunately, a huge number of people think that true love is the same thing as the feeling of being "in love" - and that's a big reason why millions of relationships between men and women are messed up. It's important to understand that it's relatively easy to get the feeling of being "in love" while dating - some people even get it without dating (a crush or infatuation).

If true love is just a feeling, feelings come and go. But true love doesn't come and go according to the Bible. A paraphrase of 1 Corinthians, chapter 13, verses 4-8 is: Love is patient and kind. It isn't jealous, rude, selfish, or easily angered. It keeps no record of wrongs. It finds no joy in evil, but rejoices in what's right. It's supportive, loyal, hopeful, and trusting. It never fails.

Unlike the feeling of being "in love", true love usually develops slowly over a significant period of time (often years). True love is so much more than just the feeling of being "in love" - it's a lifelong commitment. When you say that you love your significant other, you're saying that you're committed to loving them for the rest of your life - for richer, for poorer, in sickness and in health, from this day forward, until death do you part. True love lasts - it almost never fails.*

Think of it this way, if a person has true love for another person, it's like the sun - it's always there no matter what (remember that even when it's night, the sun is still there, it's just shining on the other side of the earth - and when it's cloudy outside the sun is also still there, it's just behind the clouds).

On the other hand, the feeling of being "in love" is like sunshine. Even though we would like it to be sunny every day, the truth is that the amount of sunshine changes regularly. Some days it's nice and sunny and the feeling of being "in love" is strong, on other days it's partly cloudy and the feeling of being "in love" is there but it's not very strong, and on some days it's cloudy/rainy and the feeling of being "in love" is barely there at all. I'm hoping that this explanation is helping you to see that it's possible for a person to have true love for another person and not have a strong intense feeling of being "in love" with that person at a particular moment. (If you talk with married couples, I think they'll tell you that the strength of their feeling of being "in love" changes on a regular basis.)

You may be asking yourself, "How can this guy talk about true love almost never failing when only about 6% of marriages end up being 50-year marriages?" Well, this is going to sound blunt - but my opinion is that one of the main reasons for this horrible statistic is that many couples marry when one or both of the partners don't actually have true love for the other - they only have the feeling of being "in love" . . . and unfortunately just having this feeling isn't enough to keep a marriage going for a lifetime.

So, when you hear someone say, "I don't love him or her anymore" - take it for what it usually is. It's usually someone saying that they've lost the feeling of being "in love", that they don't know how or they're not willing to make the effort required to get back the feeling of being "in love", and that they probably never had true love for their significant other to begin with - because true love almost never fails.

Over and over again through the years I have heard young women say, "My boyfriend loves me." Unfortunately, most of these women have been fooled. How could their boyfriend possibly have true love for them if their boyfriend doesn't even know what true love is?

How would you feel if you gave something of very high value in exchange for something that you thought had a very high value - and you later found out that what you received was worthless? Angry? Betrayed? Outraged? Depressed? How do you think that millions of unmarried young women feel after finding out that they've given their body to someone who doesn't have true love for them?**

It's time for young women to rise up and refuse to accept this fake love from young men who aren't living their lives for Christ. Young women need to realize that many men who aren't living their lives for Christ view women as sex objects - something to be used for their sexual gratification. I'm sorry if this sounds insulting - but it's time for many young women to wake up, wise up, and not be fooled. It's time for teenage women to use their teenage years to develop a close relationship with Jesus Christ instead of spending too much valuable time trying to develop a relationship with a young man.

It's also time for teenage men to use their teenage years to develop a close relationship with Jesus Christ instead of spending too much valuable time trying to develop a relationship with a young woman. In addition, it's time for teenage men to stop treating young women as sex objects and telling them that they "love" them in order to get sex.

The following comment was posted by a teen in response to reading this chapter:

"So true - what we need is love - real love. Without an intimate relationship with God, we don't have real love in our hearts so it isn't there to give - it will always be a corrupted version that we learn from our parents, friends, previous relationships, magazines, TV, music, and so on. Only God's love is true and pure - and when we cultivate a relationship with Him then we experience His love to know for ourselves and to give to others. Everything else is a miserable copycat out for self.

I agree - I see so many young girls selling themselves short in the name of acceptance and love. They are looking in all the wrong places - places that will leave deep wounds that will cause pain for years to come. If I only knew then what I know now. If anything, I've learned from all my screw-ups is just how perfect, powerful and amazing the love of God is."

*Please keep in mind that when I say that true love almost never fails, I'm not saying that a person should always remain married to a person who emotionally and/or physically abuses them, who cheats on them, or who abandons them. Very sadly it's true that true love for another person can be destroyed by a husband's or a wife's sinful words and actions. But divorce should only happen in extreme situations and after close consultation with God and intensive counseling.

**Please remember that if you've given your body to someone else without being married - God still loves you deeply and He forgives all things.

"People who understand what true love is are much more likely to be able to give it and find it."

18

. . . the danger of hearing or saying the words "I love you"

"Only say these words to someone for whom you have true love"

I heard the words "I love you" about two months after I started dating my first wife. I didn't know it at the time, but my first reaction was the right reaction - I said something like, "It's only been two months, you can't know that you love someone after two months."

But it didn't take long for my head to start swimming - in fact as I walked back to my dorm at college I jumped up in the air and said, "She loves me!" Instead of seeing someone telling me that they loved me after two months as a danger sign, I was really happy. I was completely fooled by her words and I started to get the feeling of being "in love." In fact, I made the mistake of telling her that I loved her after about five months of dating. Unfortunately, her definition of true love and my definition of true love were not the same - and she ended what was supposed to be a lifelong loving marriage relationship by divorcing me after ten years.

So, I beg you, before you say those words - please be sure that you understand what true love is. Don't say them unless you really mean them - unless you're willing to make a lifelong commitment to the person who you're saying them to.

Also, please be suspicious of anyone who says "I love you" when they have been dating you for less than a year. Ask them what they mean when they say "I love you" and share what the words mean to you - and don't give in to the pressure to say those words back just because someone has said them to you.

Please don't fall into the same horrible trap that I fell into.

Question: How can I tell if my significant other has true love for me?

This is a tough question because often it's difficult to tell if your significant other just has the feeling of being "in love" or has true love for you. Here are a few suggestions for telling the difference between the two: 1. As I mentioned earlier, true love usually doesn't develop quickly (crushes, infatuations, and obsessions develop quickly). 2. True love stands the test of time, it lasts. 3. True love has the qualities described in 1 Corinthians Chapter 13. 4. A person who has true love for you wants to remain sexually pure until marriage because they know based upon God's word that it's a good choice and that it's the best thing for your future together.

Reflection: What were the most important points to you in Chapter 16, 17, and 18?

"A couple must have mutual trust and respect before they can develop mutual true love."

19

. . . it's fine to be single

"Remember, in the eyes of God, people who are single are just as precious as those who are married"

I can almost hear you saying, "What? Not get married? Are you kidding me?" In the Bible, the Apostle Paul makes it pretty clear in 1 Corinthians, chapter 7, verse 8 that it's perfectly OK to be single. His reason for saying this is that a married person is concerned about pleasing his wife or her husband and the family - and that can make him or her less concerned about pleasing God.

The fact is that it's perfectly fine to be single. Some people are more likely to be happy single and others are more likely to be happy married.

It's much better to remain single than to marry before you or your significant other is ready to be married - and it's also much better to remain single than to marry someone who you know that God doesn't want you to marry. Couples in millions of unhappy marriages will tell you that this is true.

Reflection: What's your reaction to this chapter? Can you imagine yourself staying single if you don't find a person who God wants you to marry? Do you think that it's possible for a single person to live a happy fulfilling life? If not, why not? If so, how?

"While you're single is a great time to put in the effort required to develop a close unshakable loving relationship with God."

"Many people make choices before dating, during dating and before marriage mainly based upon feelings (without much thought and prayer) - and unfortunately these choices are often bad choices."

Notes:

20

. . . keeping the feeling of being "in love" at a high level in marriage takes a lot of effort

"Making the daily effort to keep the feeling of being 'in love' is definitely worth it"

Most couples who have the strong feeling of being "in love" during dating don't think that it's going to take much effort to keep that same feeling going after marriage.*

It's quite a shock to these couples after marriage when they don't feel as "in love" as they once did (because everyone is somewhat of a pain to live with) and they realize how much effort is required to keep the feeling of being "in love" at a high level.

I was reminded of the effort that's required to maintain this feeling when I watched the season finale of the reality show where people get voted off of an island. It was a close competition and a tie breaker of fire building was needed to decide who would be invited to the final tribal council. One contestant carefully nurtured the spark that he started with flint and steel, gradually blowing on it and adding small twigs until it became a roaring fire that burnt through the string to win the competition. Just like the contestant, both people in a marriage relationship need to make a daily effort to keep the fire of feeling "in love" burning.

Several authors have written excellent books on the subject of the importance of meeting the needs of your husband or wife and showing concern and respect for them through words and actions on a daily basis. My favorite is *Fall in Love Stay in Love* by Dr. Willard F. Harley, Jr. Please find a way to carefully read this entire book - get it from the library, order it online, borrow it from a friend, do whatever's necessary (that's legal). It's 251 pages long, but it's packed with good information. I think that the divorce rate in our society could be reduced significantly if everyone followed the principles of this book in their marriage.

One of the best pieces of marital advice that I ever received came from the best boss I ever had. He told me, "When I don't feel loving towards my wife, I try to do loving things for her and that makes me feel more loving." In other words, his effort helped both him and his wife to keep the feeling of being "in love."

*I've included this chapter because if you decide to get married one day, it's very important that you understand that keeping the feeling of being "in love" requires lifelong effort and that the book *Fall in Love Stay in Love* clearly explains how to do it.

<u>Reflection:</u> If you get married one day, what's your plan for keeping the feeling of being "in love" in the marriage?

"Pretty much anything that's worthwhile takes time and effort - including creating and maintaining a healthy positive relationship."

21

. . . how to make the decision whether or not to get married

"God should be a big part of every important decision made by a Christian"

I used to think that having true love for another person was a good enough reason to get married. I mean what else is there that's really important? Unfortunately, I learned the hard way through divorce that this alone wasn't a good enough reason to get married and that having true love often clouds a person's thinking prior to marriage. Cloudy thinking (not thinking clearly) can make you rush into a marriage decision, blind you from seeing serious problems in the person you're dating, cause you to ignore or minimize these problems, or cause you to pay no attention to danger signs.

The fact is that many, many people aren't spiritually, emotionally, and/or financially ready to get married. Many people make the decision to get married way too quickly without much thought and/or prayer because they have the strong feeling of being "in love." A quick decision is often a bad decision.

The decision to get married is a really big decision in your life. It's not one to be taken lightly. Your happiness on earth depends a lot upon whether or not you marry a person who God wants you to marry. It's the most important decision that you'll ever make, except for your decision to become a Christian.

Whenever you make any type of important decision, you need to take it to God in prayer repeatedly. You need to ask Him for wisdom and guidance. This is especially true when considering marriage. You need to talk to God about the decision over a long period of time (months, if not longer). You need to take time to listen to God speaking to you during your prayer time and you also need to read your Bible on a regular basis (1 Corinthians is a good book to read when you're considering marriage).

The following is a long list of hard questions, possibly unpleasant questions, which I suggest that you and your significant other prayerfully consider as you go through the process of deciding whether or not God wants you to get married:

- Has your significant other demonstrated, without a doubt, that they're a keeper? Are you, without a doubt, a keeper?

- Will marrying you help your significant other become closer to Christ? Will marrying your significant other help you become closer to Christ?

- Do you think that you need to change your significant other or does your significant other think that they need to change you? (this is a danger sign because true love is unconditional and rarely do people actually change)

- Have you treated each other with a high level of concern and respect in both words and actions during your dating relationship?

- Have both of you consistently demonstrated respect for other people in words and actions during your dating relationship?

- Are you both willing to make the required effort to grow spiritually/personally/emotionally throughout life?

- Have both of you completed your education and have at least two years of work experience under your belts? Have both of you taken care of yourself alone for at least a year? - in other words, do you both know how to cook, clean, wash clothes, etc.?

- Are either of you too selfish to be married? Marriage requires putting the other person first most of the time - which is a shock to many people (please see Chapter 24)

- Do both of you have the same definition of true love? In other words, are both of you willing to make an "as long as I shall live" commitment to each other instead of a selfish "as long as I feel in love" commitment?

- Do you both agree to do whatever it takes to avoid divorce and that divorce will not even be an option?

- Do you have true love for each other or does one or both of you just have the feeling of being "in love?"

- Do you have true love for each other or does one or both of you just "love feeling loved?" Are one or both of you just "in lust?"

- Are you "in love" with the lifestyle that your significant other can provide for you after marriage (remember that money can't buy happiness)? Is your significant other "in love" with the lifestyle that you can provide for him or her after marriage?

- Are you "in love" with who your significant could become (for example, a person with an important job) instead of who they're now? Is your significant other "in love" with who you could become instead of who you are now?

- In addition to having true love for each other, do both of you feel "in love?" In other words, do you have strong romantic feelings for each other? Is the chemistry there - do you really "click" with each other? Do other people notice that you have chemistry with each other?

- Has your significant other tried to control you while dating by telling you want to do, what to wear, or by trying to keep you away from your Christian friends? Have you tried to control your significant other?

- Are you or your significant other trying to get away from parents/guardians by getting married?

- Are you trying to save your significant other through marriage or do you want to be saved through marriage?

- Does your significant other treat you like a child or do you treat your significant other like a child?

- Are you or your significant other weak and have the desire to be taken care of through marriage? (Sorry if the last several questions sounded especially insulting, but marriage is supposed to be an interdependent relationship between two strong people - not a relationship with one person who's completely dependent upon the other or with one person who dominates or controls the other.)

- Are your personalities fully compatible? (They say that opposites such as introverts and extroverts sometimes attract, but people with similar personalities are more likely to stay together in marriage.)

- Does one or both of you have an idealized view of what marriage is going to be like? Do both of you have the same expectations for marriage? (Some people think that everything is going to be perfect after marriage instead of realizing that almost everyone is somewhat of a pain to live with, that marriage has its ups and downs, and that keeping the feeling of being "in love" at a high level takes a lot of effort.)

- Do you have lots and lots in common? (recreational interests, hobbies, lifestyle that you're accustomed to, values, intellectual level, political views, work ethic, etc.)

- Have both of you read this book and the book *Fall in Love Stay in Love* by Dr. Willard F. Harley, Jr. cover to cover?

- Based upon the principles in Dr. Harley's book, after you're married:

  - are both of you willing and able to communicate your needs to each other on a daily basis?

  - are both of you committed to doing your best to meet the needs of each other on a daily basis?

  - are both of you willing to make the effort required to treat your husband or wife with a high level of concern and respect in thoughts, words, and actions?

- are both of you willing to make the effort required to keep the feeling of being "in love" at a high level?

- Have you had opportunities to observe your significant other's behavior when making a good choice is hard? Has your significant other had opportunities to observe your behavior when making a good choice is hard?

- Have you allowed your significant other to see the real you during your dating relationship instead of putting on an act? Has your significant other allowed you to see the real him or her or have they just been putting on an act during your dating relationship?

- Do both of you control your tongue? (see Chapter 22)

- Do you listen well to each other? Are you both able to sense the feelings behind each other's words?

- Do both of you have good conflict resolution skills? Have you had experience resolving conflicts between each other in a calm constructive way while dating?

- Are both of you able to express your negative thoughts and feelings in a constructive manner?

- Have you communicated well (constructive, honest, open, and direct) during your dating relationship? Have you been able to have "real" communication that includes sharing negative thoughts and feelings or has everything been sugarcoated?

- Do either of you ridicule the actions, thoughts, or feelings of the other?

- Do both of you have a positive attitude almost all of the

time? (a husband or wife with a negative critical attitude towards you or others can make your life miserable)

- Have both of you shown the ability to admit mistakes/ask for forgiveness and the willingness to forgive each other? (people in a marriage relationship need to be able to admit mistakes/ask for forgiveness and forgive each other on a daily basis)

- Are you or your significant other ignoring any of the danger signs mentioned in Chapter 16 or serious problems mentioned in Chapter 1 because you have the feeling of being "in love" and want to get married?

- Do both of you want children?

- If you're blessed with children, do you agree on how the children should be raised? (in regard to discipline, faith, whether or not they'll be placed in day care, education, how much stuff they should be given, whether they should be required to do chores, etc.)

- Are you and/or your significant other able to earn what's needed to support a family?

- Are both of you willing and able to control your spending in order to remain within a budget?

- Will you and your significant other be satisfied with the lifestyle that you can afford as a couple?

- My pastor, in one of his sermons, said that it's important that people considering marriage have similar life purposes. He suggested that couples ask themselves questions like: Do you want similar things out of life?, Do you have similar goals and dreams?,

Oxen aren't very romantic, but think of yourselves as two oxen that will be yoked together - will you be pulling together in the same direction or will you be pulling in opposite directions?

- Are both of you at least 24 years of age? (as I mentioned before, statistics show that the divorce rate for people who first marry at age 24 or above is significantly lower than those who first marry below age 24)

- Has your dating relationship been pleasing to God?

- Would your marriage be pleasing to God?

- Have you attended in-depth Christian premarital counseling, which emphasizes the development of communication and constructive conflict resolution skills, with a qualified pastor or Christian counselor?

Whew! - as you can see there are many questions that need to be prayerfully considered as you go through the process of deciding whether or not to get married. It's also a very good idea to seek the counsel of Christian relatives and friends. If the majority of your Christian relatives and friends are opposed to your getting married, it's more than likely best to decide not to get married, or at the very least postpone the decision. There's no reason to rush into what could be a bad decision. If he or she's unhappy that you need more time to make a decision, it could be a danger sign - remember the verse that says "Love is patient."

(I realize this book is about teen dating, but if you follow the suggestions of becoming a keeper and dating a person who's a keeper, you may eventually be faced with the decision of whether or not to get married. Hopefully this chapter will help you to make a good well thought out decision.)

22

. . . an uncontrolled tongue not being a good thing

"No man can tame the tongue" (James, chapter 3, verse 8)

I messed up yesterday. I talked to my wife in a way that made her feel like she was being scolded. Instead of treating her like an adult and expressing my negative feelings in a calm constructive manner about a particular situation, I acted like she was the child and I was the parent - not a good way to treat her with respect and to make her feel loved. Thankfully, we were able to talk it out and I told her that I was sorry about the disrespectful way I had expressed my feelings. She forgave me.

The reason I brought this up is to give you an example that, even after many years of marriage, I'm still making mistakes using my tongue.* Unfortunately it's a daily battle that sometimes the tongue wins. The uncontrolled tongue does a huge amount of damage to both dating and marriage relationships. Think about all of the uncaring words that are spoken between husbands and wives - words that would never be said, especially in the way that they're often said, if they were keeping their marriage vow (their promise to God) to love, honor, and cherish their husband or wife.

At this point in his life, my teenage son thinks that he should express what's on his mind when it's on his mind. He thinks that holding things in isn't good for him - you know, like he might develop stomach problems. We've tried to explain to him that sometimes things need to left unsaid or at the very least not be said until everyone has had a chance to cool off and a calm respectful conversation can take place. We've tried to teach our children to ask themselves questions in their minds before saying something. Questions like: 1. Is it true? 2. Is it necessary? 3. Will saying it make the situation better? 4. Does God want me to say it? 5. How can I say what needs to be said in a way that's as positive as possible? (In other words, how can I say what needs to be said in love?) 6. Is this the right time and place to say it?

Reality is that you can't control your tongue on your own - it's simply too powerful. James, chapter 3, verses 6 and 7 refers to the tongue as a fire that corrupts. I've found that it's helpful to ask God in prayer every day for help controlling my tongue.

This chapter was included because many people don't realize how important it is to use their tongue wisely and how much damage an uncontrolled tongue can cause to relationships. You may be forgiven after you say something without thinking, but it sometimes takes a long time for the damage to be repaired. I encourage you to learn along with me how to control your tongue and to use it in a positive manner to build healthy relationships in your life.

*Unfortunately, the tongue tends to loosen when you move from dating (an uncommitted relationship) to marriage (a committed relationship). Over the years I've been shocked and saddened to hear how some married couples talk to each other.

"Wisdom is divided into two parts: 1) having a great deal to say 2) not saying it." - Anonymous

"I would say more, but I can't seem to get my foot out of my mouth."

23

. . . three dangerous attitudes

"We love each other so much, it'll always be this way, and we'll never get divorced"

As I mentioned before, I used to have the "divorce won't happen to me" attitude. Never in my wildest dreams did I ever imagine being divorced in my lifetime. After all, I came from a good family with parents committed to each other, I was a Christian, I tried to be a nice person, I tried to meet her needs, and I thought we had true love for each other. Even when things got rough, I told myself that everything was eventually going to be all right because we loved each other.

Unfortunately, my first marriage still ended in divorce. The main problems were that at the time of our marriage neither she nor I was a keeper and we had different definitions of true love. (Looking back at the marriage, I now realize that we also didn't put enough effort into keeping the feeling of being "in love" as described in Chapter 20.)

The truth is that the "divorce won't happen to me" attitude is dangerous because it can cause you to make a bad choice of a marriage partner and after marriage it can cause you to think that you don't need to put much effort into keeping the feeling of being "in love." A lifelong loving Christian marriage takes two people deeply committed to each other, a willingness to grow up (ouch) - as well as a lot of hard work, love, and forgiveness.

Another dangerous attitude is "divorce is no big deal." Please don't let seeing celebrities go through one divorce after another fool you into thinking that divorce is no big deal. As I stressed in Chapter 3, it's a big deal for almost everyone who gets divorced.

The reason why the "divorce is no big deal" attitude is so dangerous is that people with this attitude are less likely to carefully go through the decision-making process described in Chapter 21 and are more likely to make a bad marriage decision.

And finally, the "I know it all" attitude is dangerous. Have you ever noticed that regardless of our age many of us, including myself, at times seem to think we "know it all?" Unfortunately, a good number of teens that I've talked with over the years have this attitude. The truth is that none of us "know it all" and that life is supposed to be a lifelong learning and growing process.

The danger is that people with this attitude are more likely to stop learning and stop trying to grow spiritually, personally, and emotionally. Unfortunately, these people often learn their lessons the hard way by making bad choices that affect them for a long period of time.

My hope is that reading this book will help you to not have any of these attitudes.

Reflection: Do you have any of these attitudes? If so, what can you do to stop having it?

24

. . . the number one sin that we have to battle daily - selfishness

"Contrary to popular belief, the best possible life isn't found in personal gain and personal pleasure - it's found in loving God and loving others."

We're naturally selfish - we're concerned about having good food in our belly, nice clothes on our back, a solid roof over our heads, all kinds of "stuff", and having lots of fun. However, too much selfishness is destructive to yourself and to your relationships with others. Face it, we live in a "Me First" society - people want what they want when they want it. This is exactly the opposite of how God wants us to live. He actually wants us to forget about ourselves and focus on loving Him and on loving others. True joy that lasts is never found in selfishness - it's found in loving God and loving others.

Here's a quick example of what I'm trying to communicate: I really enjoy amusement parks and when our family goes, we stay from opening to close. Now that we have children, my main source of joy is no longer from the excitement of riding the rides that I want to ride (selfishness) - instead it's from seeing the joy on their faces as they enjoy themselves riding the rides. My focus is off of myself. My joy comes from loving them by going on the rides that they want to ride. I get more joy watching them go around in circles on the little kiddie airplanes than I do riding the fastest, scariest ride.

Whether we're single or married, we need to realize that the number one sin that we're going to have to battle on a daily basis is selfishness. We go through most of our single life with ourselves as our #1 concern. If we get married, all of a sudden after a few words said by a pastor, someone else that we love is supposed to be our #1 concern. We're now #2. (If God blesses you with children, we become an even lower priority.) When we get married, we make a vow (promise) to God to love, honor, and cherish our lifelong mate regardless of whether we feel like doing it and regardless of what we receive in return.

To many people who get married, having to put someone else first is a big shock - it means that they can no longer say or do whatever they want whenever they want. Old habits are often slow to die. It means that they have to grow up (sorry if this sounds insulting). I have to confess that there are times when I resent having to put my wife first and sometimes, I fail to put her first. I have to ask God to forgive me for the resentment/ failures and to help me focus on my daily commitment - loving my wife in a way that's pleasing to Him.

So, "How do you go about battling selfishness on a daily basis?" Regardless of what sin you're battling, it's always best to turn to our source of strength - God, Our Lord and Savior Jesus Christ, and the Holy Spirit. We need to pray every day asking for help and strength in our battle against selfishness. I realize that every day seems like a bit much - but we need to remember that selfishness is a sin that we'll battle daily throughout our lives.

(My students and I came up with a somewhat silly but fun idea to help people in families recognize selfishness - when someone says something that's just out and out selfish, for example bragging about how great they are, the other people in the family together say "goy!" in a funny way. Goy! stands for "get off yourself." When someone is demanding their own way, family members give them a "goy!" Usually everyone starts laughing after the word is said. It can help people in a family to recognize when they're being selfish in a positive way. (Talk over this idea with your family and see if they want to try it.)

25

. . . the ten main causes of divorce

"True love lasts - it almost never fails."

Over the years I've developed the following list of what I think are the main causes of divorce (in no particular order)*:

1. The husband and/or the wife didn't take the time necessary to go on the journey of preparing themselves for dating and marriage before marriage - which means that one or both of them were not ready to be married.

2. One or both people not being a keeper

3. One or both people not having true love for the other, not knowing what true love is, or possibly not understanding that even happily married couples don't have the strong feeling of being "in love" all the time. (Many couples don't realize that emotions are heightened while dating because they're in an uncommitted insecure relationship - everything seems extremely exciting and intense. They misinterpret the natural reduction of emotions that takes place in marriage, a committed secure relationship, as "we don't love each other the way we used to" or "we're not 'in love' anymore.") Please remember that true love is much more than just a feeling, it's a lifelong commitment.

4. Selfishness - which often shows itself through uncaring words and actions, an unwillingness to put the needs of your husband or wife first, and an unwillingness to grow up. People who are selfish often seek a divorce because they're not getting what they want from their husband or wife (affection, attention, possessions, lifestyle, excitement, respect, etc.). They don't

understand that when they got married, they made a covenant (a promise to their husband or wife and to God) that they would love their husband or wife regardless of what they receive back from them (this covenant is supposed to be only broken after consulting with God and after intense professional counseling in situations of abuse, abandonment, or adultery).

5. Too high of expectations - many couples expect the strong "we're so in love" feeling they had before marriage to continue throughout marriage without much effort. They expect their husband or wife to meet all of their needs. They truly believe that they'll "live happily ever after." When they have conflicts, which are going to happen in any relationship, they possibly even start thinking, "we don't love each other anymore." The truth is that any marriage relationship has ups and downs and the intensity of the feeling of being "in love" between husband and wife changes regularly with these ups and downs. True love combined with a willingness to put in the effort required to make the other person feel loved (described in #6) is what keeps a marriage going during these down times.

6. Unwillingness of one or both people to make the effort required on a daily basis to keep the feeling of being "in love." My pastor said that it's amazing the amount of effort that couples are willing to put into a relationship while dating and how little effort they're willing to put into a relationship after marriage. He said that relationships are like grass - they need watering (quality time together, date nights, etc.) to stay green and healthy. Keeping a relationship strong takes work and maintenance as discussed in Chapter 20.

7. Failure of one or both people to treat the other with a high level of concern and respect in words and actions on a consistent basis

8. Power struggles - these occur when one or both people selfishly try to dominate or control the other in order to have their own way (God wants husbands and wives to treat each other with mutual love and respect.)

9. Poor communication and conflict resolution skills - many couples don't know how to communicate well and how to resolve conflicts in a calm constructive way that doesn't damage the relationship. (all premarital counseling should include training to improve communication and conflict resolution skills)

10. One or both people being unable or unwilling to control their spending

*Of course, divorce often occurs from a mixture of these causes.

Question: _Is it OK to live together?_

The number of unmarried couples living together has skyrocketed during the past few decades. Many of these couples think that living together isn't wrong because "pretty much everyone is doing it." Sadly, it's become rare to attend a wedding of a couple who hasn't lived together.

I've heard lots of reasons why people live together including, "It's helping us to save up for a house", "We want to work for a few years before we get married", "He's not ready to make a commitment", "We want to be sure that we're compatible", "We're going to get married eventually, we're just not sure when", etc.

Unfortunately, the truth is that living together is a mistake - no matter how many people are doing it. That's not my opinion, it's God's.** It's almost impossible for a couple to obey God when He says, "Flee from sexual immorality" in 1 Corinthians, chapter 6, verse 18 and live together at the same time. Statistics back up God's position on this matter. Most studies show that couples who live together before marriage are more likely to get divorced than couples who don't and couples who live together before marriage are more likely to be unhappy in their marriage.

If your significant other wants to live with you before marriage, it's a sign that he or she's a person that God doesn't want you to marry (because he or she doesn't have the Godly character of a keeper).

**God will forgive you for any mistake if you turn to Him.

Reflection: What were the most important points that you want to remember from Chapter 21 through Chapter 25?

"People who use living together as a test drive before marriage are much more likely to have a major wreck after marriage - divorce."

"It's true that a selfish person may be happy for a short period of time, but I've never met a selfish person who's been happy, content, and fulfilled throughout their entire life."

"Selfishness is like a drought to a relationship - it eventually makes it wither."

Epilogue

. . . a cultural revolution being needed

We need a cultural revolution in order to significantly reduce the divorce rate in our society. My proposed revolution may sound extreme - but I'm suggesting that teens first take the time to develop a close relationship with Jesus Christ before trying to develop a relationship with a member of the opposite sex. Specifically, I'm suggesting that teens become a keeper and be at least a freshman in high school before group dating. I'm also suggesting that teens who are keepers consider waiting until they're a junior or a senior in high school before they start one-on-one dating. Choosing not to date in high school is a good choice for many teens. *Unfortunately, the pandemic of divorce needs strong medicine.*

I can almost hear younger teens screaming things like: "What are we going to do for fun?, What are we going to do on the weekends?, That would make life so boring., All the good ones will be gone by then!, Did you actually suggest that it's OK not to date in high school?" And I can almost hear the parents and grandparents screaming: "I dated at an early age and it turned out just fine. I'm going to let my child/grandchild do the same. Don't suggest that my child/grandchild should wait to date one-on-one until they're a junior or a senior in high school - I think that's too long to wait!"

Before everyone gets themselves too worked up, here's what the cultural revolution would look like if it's achieved:

A dramatic increase in the number of:

* teens who are keepers

95

- teens waiting until they're a keeper before they date

- teen keepers who will only date other teen keepers

- teens using the "Dating with God" approach to dating

- teens participating in group dating*

- wholesome and fun recreational activities available for teens on Friday and Saturday nights at a reasonable cost

- people in a lifelong loving Christian marriage relationship

A dramatic decrease in the:

- number of teens who are participating in one-on-one dating using the "Dating without God" approach

- amount of pain and anguish caused by broken hearts

- number of teens with sexually transmitted diseases (The statistics are absolutely shocking. A Center for Disease Control study shows that 25% of sexually active teen girls have an STD. They don't seem to realize or don't seem to care that they're taking a high risk of damaging their health. Sadly, many of these teens have the "It's not going to happen to me" attitude until they get an STD.)

- divorce rate

Here are some possible suggestions for how to make this cultural revolution happen:

- inspire teens to complete the journey of preparing

themselves for dating through learning and spiritual/personal/emotional growth by helping them to picture how wonderful a lifelong loving Christian marriage could be

- educate teens about the dangers of sexually transmitted diseases

- ask parents to strongly encourage their teen to become a keeper before they date and to only date another keeper

- ask parents to consider not allowing their teens below a freshman in high school to participate in group or one-on-one dating (as you read in Chapter 9 - the later the better)

- ask parents to consider allowing only group dating of six or more people while their teen is a freshman or a sophomore in high school* (time alone as a couple should be minimized)

- ask parents to consider allowing their high school teens to only date someone who's no more than two grade levels higher than their year in school (for example, a sophomore could date no higher than a senior - a junior could date no higher than a freshman in college, etc. The purpose of this suggestion is to protect teens from being taken advantage of by smooth talking older teens and young adults.)

- ask churches to make developing youth into keepers their #1 priority

- ask people who read this book to consider telling their friends and family about it in person or through social media (suggest to friends and family that they go to

97

truelovelasts.org to read a few excerpts from the book (especially the excerpt about true love), writing an online review of this book at their favorite bookseller's website, suggesting to your youth pastor that your youth group study this book, or asking your local library or church library to put the book on their shelves (we will send a book at no charge if the library or church sends a request to TLLinfo@aol.com.)

- ask churches, the "Y", other Christian organizations, and recreation departments to work together to provide as many as possible wholesome and fun recreational programs/activities at a reasonable cost on Friday and Saturday nights as an alternative to one-on-one dating

*Please don't think for a minute that "group dating just isn't realistic" - we know of a youth pastor and his wife who went to the prom with his youth group. That's right, over twenty couples including the youth pastor and his wife went to a fancy dinner and then to the prom together. It was a great group date that will always be remembered.

Reflection: What's your reaction to the suggested cultural revolution? What parts of it do you agree with? What parts of it don't you agree with? What's the most important thing that you think needs to be done in order to make it happen?

Final Word to Girls

The lives of more and more teen girls are spinning out of control. It's hard to believe that so many girls around the world are dating at an early age and are giving their bodies before marriage to someone else for fun, because they think they have true love for someone, because they think someone has true love for them, or because they hope they'll get true love if they do so. (I read an article in the newspaper that said about 33% of women in the United States becomes pregnant before the age of 20 . . . what a sad statistic for the women, but even more so for the children - many of whom will grow up without a constant strong loving father figure in their lives.)

Many girls move from one relationship to another searching for true love. They don't know that they're looking for true love in all the wrong places. They don't realize that they're damaging their emotions (please see Chapter 8). They don't understand that they're setting themselves up for a wide variety of life changing events such as:

- getting a sexually transmitted disease* (It's not a joke, it's a horrible problem - a government agency estimates that there are over 19 million new STD infections each year and about half of these infections are in teens and young adults. The agency also estimates that about 24,000 women in the United States become infertile each year because of an STD.)

- becoming a mother without being married*

- realizing that the person who you gave your body to doesn't have true love for you*

- realizing that you don't have true love for the person who you gave your body to*

- being in an emotionally and/or physically abusive dating relationship

- being in an unhappy unloving marriage relationship

- being divorced

- having a broken heart

I hope this book has given you some good information about dating from a Christian perspective that you can use to maximize the possibility that you'll have a lifelong loving Christian marriage if you decide to get married one day. I also hope that reading this book will help you to have high standards for yourself and for the person who you decide to date.

Here are some final words that you've probably already heard from someone, but I need to make sure: You need to know that many men are selfish/immature and they want to use your body for their pleasure. Many will tell you almost anything (the most effective being "I love you") in order to get what they want. I realize that no one likes to be told to "wake up", but you need to "wake up" to these facts if you haven't already done so.

Another thing you need to know is that unfortunately, "good" men (keepers) are few and far between - and a big part of the reason for this is that women's standards for who is acceptable dating material aren't high enough. It seems that many women are willing to date almost anyone they like or feel attracted to. In contrast, God wants you to be very selective about who you date because He truly loves you and wants only the very best for you. Quite frankly, you need to know that dating a man that God doesn't want you to date can damage your life - especially if you end up marrying him.

If women are strong and have high standards - this will help to force men to grow up. It's not easy being a strong woman of God in our society - but He will bless you if you live your life for Him!

*Please remember that God loves you no matter what. His love is unconditional. As long as you're alive it's not too late to turn to Him, ask Him for forgiveness, and start living your life for Him.

My hope is that reading this book has helped to inspire you to continue on the journey of preparing yourself for dating. Please see the Appendix starting on p. 105 for a variety of information including tips for attracting a keeper, dating questions and answers, and a list of recommended books that can help you to continue on the journey.

<u>Reflection:</u> Are you willing to put in the effort that's required throughout life in order to be a strong woman of God? Do you believe that being a strong woman of God will help you to have the best possible life?

"Guard your heart - don't just give it away to anybody."

"If you get engaged one day, continue to use the engagement time to find out what your significant other is really like - just like you did while you were dating. The stress of all the planning and preparation that takes place during engagement often helps to reveal what your significant other is really like (including what their domestic personality is like). If you see a danger sign during engagement, please don't just ignore it - be strong and immediately get professional counseling. The outcome of counseling may be to continue on with the wedding as planned, postpone it or to cancel it. A broken engagement is much better than a broken marriage."

Notes:

Final Word to Guys

I hope this book has given you some good information about dating from a Christian perspective that you can use to maximize the possibility that you'll have a lifelong loving Christian marriage if you decide to get married one day. I also hope that reading this book will help you to have high standards for yourself and for the person who you decide to date.

Here are some final words that you've probably already heard from someone, but I need to make sure: You need to know that many women are selfish/immature and they desperately want someone to love them - someone to meet their emotional and other needs. Many will tell you almost anything (the most effective being "I love you") and are willing to give you their bodies before marriage in order to get what they want. I realize that no one likes to be told to "wake up," but you need to "wake up" to these facts before you fall into their trap.

Another thing you need to know is that unfortunately "good" women (keepers) are hard to find - and a big part of the reason for this is that men's standards for who is acceptable dating material aren't high enough. It seems that many men are willing to date almost anyone with good looks. In contrast, God wants you to be very selective about who you date because He truly loves you and wants only the very best for you. The Bible says in the book of Proverbs, chapter 31, verse 10 that a good wife is a precious treasure.

Quite frankly, you need to know that dating the wrong woman can severely damage your life. Even just one date can be dangerous. I know this may sound hard to believe, but here's how: some women are so attractive on the outside that you can't see or you ignore their serious problems, you completely forget that beauty on the inside (Godly character) is what you mainly should be looking for - and sadly you end up marrying a person who God doesn't want you to marry. Unfortunately, unhappiness and divorce are often the result of this bad choice.

If men are strong and have high standards - this will help to force women to grow up. It's not easy being a strong man of God in our society - but He will bless you if you live your life for Him!

My hope is that reading this book has helped to inspire you to continue on the journey of preparing yourself for dating. Please see the Appendix starting on p. 105 for a variety of information including tips for attracting a keeper, dating questions and answers, and a list of recommended books that can help you to continue on the journey.

<u>Reflection:</u> Are you willing to put in the effort that's required throughout life in order to be a strong man of God? Do you believe that being a strong man of God will help you to have the best possible life?

"Have you noticed that in today's society the word love is way overused? We love our sports teams, our car, our pet, our favorite snack, you name it. Wouldn't it make more sense to only use the word love when we're talking about our family, our friends, or our significant other?"

Appendix

21 TIPS THAT CAN HELP YOU ATTRACT A KEEPER

1. Take the time and put in the effort to become a keeper yourself (This is the most important tip.)

2. As mentioned in Chapter 16, put yourself in as many situations as possible that will allow you to potentially come in contact with other keepers - church, church activities, church youth group activities, the library, a high school Christian club, the "Y" or other workout facilities, Bible studies, coffee shops, non-alcoholic parties, Christian bookstores, Christian concerts (be sure to wear a good pair of earplugs to protect your ears from permanent hearing loss), Christian organizations (such as Young Life, Youth for Christ, and Fellowship of Christian Athletes), church athletic teams, community service projects, mission trips, volunteer service in church, etc. Try to get to know other people as much as possible without dating

3. Be cheerful, approachable, and friendly - smile regularly to put others at ease (Let people see your positive attitude)

4. Take a real interest in getting to know others. Ask people open-ended questions about themselves in order to get them talking. Share as needed to keep the conversation going - and then ask another open-ended question

5. Be polite and kind to everyone - even to people who you don't like or enjoy being around

6. If you decide to not accept a request for a date, do it in a kind way (Being rude isn't a good choice and it doesn't help you because your reputation for rudeness will make you less approachable)

7. Be confident about yourself based upon your position as a daughter or son of God

105

8. Be humble - don't act like you think you're wonderful

9. Don't be too concerned about whether or not someone likes you

10. Have the attitude that if someone doesn't like you - they don't really know you

11. Take care of yourself by getting enough sleep (at least nine hours for teens according to the experts), exercising regularly (if approved by your doctor), and eating a healthy diet

12. Develop a good sense of humor - including the ability to laugh at your own mistakes

13. Be known as a hard worker

14. Dress well and dress modestly at the same time (Please see p. 115 for an excellent short book about clothing and modesty.)

15. Pay attention to your appearance, but don't obsess over it. Remember that hard working people with Godly character (keepers) are attracted to other hard-working people with Godly character - they're not overly concerned about looks because they know looks fade with age. If you use makeup, make sure it's not excessive. Use perfumes and colognes sparingly - if at all

16. Truly care about other people

17. Stay in close communication with God through daily prayer

18. Be patient - ask God regularly for help being patient

19. Persevere - please remember that almost nothing worthwhile is easy, ask God for strength to persevere. Don't settle

20. Don't take it personally if someone doesn't want to date you

21. Don't act desperate for a date

Dating questions and answers

In order to try to help people to make good dating choices, I've answered thousands of dating questions online and in person. The following are some of the most asked questions and answers. The wording has been changed to protect the identity of the asker. I hope that these questions and answers will help you to make good dating choices.

Q. I already know what I'm doing and I want to make my own mistakes. Why do I need to read any information and suggestions about dating?

A. Of course it's a free country and you can do pretty much whatever you want unless it's against the law. However, that doesn't mean that bad dating and marriage choices made without having good information won't have a negative effect upon your life and upon the lives of others (your significant other, children, parents, siblings, etc.). I encourage you to take the time to become as knowledgeable as possible about dating and marriage because the truth is that nobody knows it all. My opinion, based upon years of observation, is that people who put in the time and effort required to become really knowledgeable about dating and marriage are more likely to make good choices and are more likely to find true love.

Q. I like him, I think he likes me, and he's so cute. Should I ask him out?

A. Sorry, I know that it's old-fashioned, but my opinion is that this usually isn't a good idea. Some people may disagree - but I think that if he's a keeper and you're a keeper and he's interested, he'll eventually take the initiative and ask you out. Instead of asking him out or telling him that you like him, why not just act like you like him by asking him open-ended questions about things that he's interested in?

I could be wrong, but based upon your question it sounds like you're making dating choices mainly based upon whether someone likes you, you like them, and looks. Unfortunately, this approach to dating, used by most people, usually leads to a broken heart.

May I suggest that the first question to ask yourself when considering whether or not to date someone is, "Is this person a keeper?"

My suggestion is that you put in the effort necessary to become a keeper (if you're not already), forget about this guy unless he's a keeper, and eventually look for this type of guy (otherwise you're setting yourself up for a broken heart). Unfortunately, this type of man is difficult to find - but save yourself the heartache and don't settle for less.

Please remember that you want a 50-year fulfilling marriage - not a 5 or a 10-year marriage. Hope this helps!

Q. How do I get up the courage to ask a girl out?

A. It's natural to feel nervous when you're thinking about asking a woman who is a keeper out. I sure was. Pretty much everyone has the fear of rejection. I hope that this doesn't sound too harsh, but if you're having a big problem working up the courage to ask a keeper out, it's possible that you need to work on becoming a stronger person before asking her out. Practice what you're going to say and plan a good time to ask her out in-person. I know that rejection is tough for anyone to handle, but the goal is to become so strong as a person that you aren't too concerned about what other people say, do, or think - and that includes a lady who says "no" when you ask her for a date. A keeper has a positive but humble "if a person doesn't want to go on a date with me, that's OK" attitude.

Q. I'm 19 and I've never had a girlfriend. I feel like I'm so far behind my friends in terms of experience. I'm beginning to think that I'm going to be alone all my life. What should I do?

A. You're being way too hard on yourself. It's actually a good thing that you haven't had a girlfriend yet because it means that you've avoided having your heart broken. The best way to attract a keeper is to become a keeper.

Q. We spend hours and hours talking on a social media site and texting. I've only met him in person once, but I think I'm starting to fall in love with him. What should I do?

A. First of all let me explain that when someone says that they are "falling in love" it usually means that a person is starting to have the feeling of being "in love" - instead of true love which is supposed to be a lifelong commitment. Please remember that having the feeling of being "in love" is relatively easy to get - while true love involves really getting to know another person and usually takes a long period of time to develop (often years).

Please keep in mind that it's easy for a person to hide what they are really like when they mainly communicate via social media and texting. Research shows that over 50% of good communication between two people is actually nonverbal (body language, the expression on someone's face, etc.) which you don't get electronically. My suggestion is that you dramatically cut back on the time that you spend on social media and texting - and find a way to spend more time in face-to-face conversation with him as well as participating in a wide variety of wholesome activities together. This is the only way for you to get to know what he's really like and for him to get to know what you're really like. Be sure to pay special attention to how your significant other treats you and other people - and how he reacts when something goes wrong or he doesn't get what he wants.

Q. Could I possibly love someone I hardly know? I can't stop thinking about him.

A. It's highly unlikely that you have true love for someone you hardly know. It sounds like you have a bad case of infatuation. Infatuation is having the intense feeling of being "in love" very quickly - sometimes at first sight. True love is so much more than just having the feeling of being "in love" - it's supposed to be a mutual lifelong commitment. When you say that you love your significant other, you're saying that you're committed to loving them for the rest of your life. Please remember that true love lasts - it almost never fails.

Q. She dumped me. How can I get over her?

A. I'm really sorry about your heartache. One of the best ways to get over a woman is to put in the time and effort to become a keeper - if you're not one already. The good news in this bad situation is that you found out that she doesn't have true love for you. Although what you're going through is very painful, it's way better to have found this out now instead of finding it out after marriage. You may need some professional counseling to help you get over her. It's often available for a low fee through health insurance.

Q. How do I know whether or not to continue in a dating relationship?

A. A decision of whether or not to continue in a dating relationship should be made after participating in a wide variety of wholesome activities together in order to carefully find out what the person you're dating is really like and to give the person you're dating an opportunity to find out what you're really like. Please remember that many people try to hide what they are really like by putting on an act during dating. Good reasons for breaking off a dating relationship in a kind way include: the other person not treating you and/or others with respect, the other person having a serious problem, the other person not having one or more of the characteristics of a keeper, realizing that you don't have lots and lots in common after all, realizing that you don't think the same things are important in life, realizing the chemistry that you thought was there isn't there or realizing that this isn't the person you want to spend the rest of your life with.

Unfortunately, way too many people stay in a dating relationship because they don't want to be without a boyfriend or girlfriend - instead of being strong and breaking up in a kind but firm way. It's better to be lonely than it is to be dating a person who you know isn't right for you. Millions of people in unhappy relationships will agree that this statement is true.

Q. My boyfriend cheated on me, but I still love him. How do I get him back?

A. Unfortunately true love is supposed to be a mutual lifelong commitment. By cheating on you he's proven that he doesn't have true love for you. He's shown that he can't be trusted - and that most likely he will cheat on you again in the future. He's shown that he's not a keeper. I'm sorry to sound blunt - but why would you want this kind of guy back? Do you want to set yourself up for another broken heart in the future?

My suggestion is that you forget about this guy, become a keeper (if you're not already) and eventually look for a keeper. It's true that this type of guy is not easy to find, but please don't settle for less. Please don't hesitate to go to professional counseling if you need help talking through this and getting over this guy.

Q. Is love a good enough reason to marry someone?

A. Unfortunately many times not. When you say love, I'm presuming that you mean true love - love that is supposed to be a lifelong commitment, instead of just having the feeling of being "in love." In addition to being sure that you have true love for each other, you need to ask yourselves many questions like: Are both of you keepers? Do you have lots and lots of things in common? Do you have mutual true love for each other? Is their strong chemistry between the two of you? Do you have similar goals for your life together? Are the same things in life important to both of you? Do you have very similar values? Have you treated each other and others with respect during your dating relationship? Are both of you hard workers? Are both of you free of serious problems? Do both of you agree that divorce is not even an option? Do you know how you're going to pay the bills if you decide to get married? Do both of you know how to control money? Do both of you want children? Do respected adults (who are keepers) think that it's a good idea for you to get married?

Q. Why should I put in the effort to try to live my life every day as a keeper?

A. Three important reasons - #1 Living your life as a keeper will help you to have the best possible life #2 Keepers are more likely to find true love and to be able to give true love #3 Keepers are more likely to have a lifelong loving marriage if they decide to get married one day

Q. What's the best way to kiss my boyfriend in order to turn him on?

A. I wouldn't worry about it until you're married - you don't want things to get out of hand. (I also include some information about long make out sessions from pp. 62-63 in the answer.)

Q. How do I make myself look more attractive to guys?

A. A guy who is a keeper is attracted to a hard-working woman who is a keeper. Even though this type of guy isn't overly concerned with looks (because he realizes that looks fade with age) - it helps to pay attention to your appearance (but don't obsess), wear attractive modest clothing (keepers are not attracted to girls who wear immodest clothing), exercise (if your doctor says it's OK), eat a good balanced diet that minimizes fats and sugars, and get your sleep (9-10 hours for teens and 7-8 hours for young adults). The best way to become more attractive is to practice living your life as a keeper every day.

Q. How do I talk to a girl that I'm interested in?

A. I hope that the main reason you're interested in her is because you think she's a keeper. If you don't know for sure that she is, try to find a way to get to know her without dating - for example, participate in activities of the same school club or youth/young adult church group that she's in. If you have the opportunity, just say "hi" when you see her. Be pleasant and if you have a chance, get her talking about herself by asking her an open-ended (one that can't be answered yes or no) question like, "What do you like to do in your spare time?" Share something related to what she said and then ask her another question.

Q. What should I do if my boyfriend is pressuring me to have sex?

A. This is going to sound harsh, but unfortunately this is a sign that your boyfriend isn't a keeper and it's time to break up with him in a kind but firm way. Here are the reasons why:

First of all, he's not listening to God's Word. In Ephesians, chapter 5, verse 3 God says, "among you their must not be even the hint of sexual immorality." A man who loves God with all his heart obeys God whether he feels like it or not.

A boyfriend who has true love for you is willing to put aside his short-term desires for the long-term health of the relationship. (please keep in mind that statistics show that married couples who had pre-marital sex are more likely to eventually get divorced).

And finally, a boyfriend who respects you would never choose to pressure you in such a way. Respect is a crucial part of the foundation of any lasting relationship.

Q. What should I do next after reading *Straight Talk About Teen Dating*?

A. Take action by using the information/suggestions in the book. Many people who read the book realize that there are some characteristics of a keeper that they need to work on and that now is a great time for them to put in the time and effort required to fully develop those characteristics.

Some people who read the book decide that they need to put in the energy required to find a few real Christian friends to go through life together with - friends who will help and encourage them to grow in their faith - friends to whom they can be mutually accountable. Some people find these real friends in a small group at church.

Many people decide to read other books on the recommended book list on p. 115. And finally, a good number of people who read the book decide to practice using the "21 tips that can help you attract a keeper" on p. 105.

Recommended books for your journey

The following books have been carefully selected with the hope that they will help you on your journey of preparing yourself for dating. Books are recommended for all ages unless otherwise noted.

Fall in Love Stay in Love by Dr. Willard F. Harley, Jr.

. . . can help you learn how to keep the strong feeling of being "in love" as much as possible during marriage

The Look: Does God Really Care What I Wear? by Nancy Leigh DeMoss

. . . a 53-page booklet that will help you to think about clothing and modesty from God's perspective

This Is Now: A Girl-to-Girl Devotional for Teens compiled by Patti M. Hummel

. . . confronts the real-life issues and challenges facing teenage girls

The Myth of the Submissive Christian Woman: Walking with God without Being Stepped On by Others by Brenda Waggoner

. . . explains how submission from a biblical perspective isn't what many people think it is - recommended for high school age and up

Couple Skills: Making Your Relationship Work by Matthew McKay

. . . will help you to improve your communication skills - recommended for high school age and up

We Can Work It Out: How to Solve Conflicts, Save Your Marriage by C. Notarius and Howard Markman

. . . will help you to improve your conflict resolution skills - recommended for high school age and up

Group Dating: 301 Ideas by Blair Tolman, Tristan Tolman, and Kelli Weaver

. . . can spark your imagination for wholesome and fun group dating activities

When God Writes Your Love Story (Expanded Edition): The Ultimate Guide to Guy/Girl Relationships by Eric Ludy and Leslie Ludy

. . . will help you to become or remain the type of person God wants you to date

Sex is Not the Problem (Lust Is): Sexual Purity in a Lust-Saturated World by Joshua Harris

. . . gets to the heart of our struggles against lust - we're weak and we need to depend upon God . . . it also includes excellent practical advice for battling lust

Getting Ready for Marriage Workbook - How to Really get to Know the Person You're Going to Marry by Jerry Hardin and Dianne Sloan

. . . can help couples to make a good decision about whether or not to get married - recommended for couples considering engagement or engaged couples

Growing Your Faith: How to Mature in Christ by Gerald Bridges

. . . will help you learn how to grow spiritually - recommended for high school age and up

God, Help Me Pray!: E-mails to God on the Teaching of Prayer for Teachers and New Christians by Jerry L. Parks

. . . a 66-page book filled with practical information about how to talk with God

Hearing the Master's Voice: The Comfort and Confidence of Knowing God's Will by Robert Jeffress

. . . will help you to determine God's will as you make important decisions in your life - recommended for high school age and up

Battlefield of the Mind for Teens: Winning the Battle in Your Mind by Joyce Meyer with Todd Hafer

. . . will help you to fight off temptations and win the battle in your mind between good and evil

Josh McDowell's One Year Book of Youth Devotions by Josh McDowell and Bob Hostetler

. . . a devotional book that will help you to use God's Word on a daily basis

How to stay Christian in High School by Steve Gerali

. . . will help you to resist peer pressure and live your life for Christ in high school

Can I Be a Christian Without Being Weird? by Kevin Johnson

. . . a devotional book, written for early teens, that will help you to know God and to become a follower of Jesus Christ

God Allows U-Turns for Teens: The Choices We Make Change the Story of Our Life by Allison Bottke and Cheryll Hutchings

. . . proves that it's never too late to turn your life around

True Volume 1: Real stories about God showing up in the lives of teens by Irene Dunlap

. . . will help you to clearly see that God is with you always and that He will help you through anything if you put your faith and trust in Him

Complete Idiot's Guide to Money for Teens by Susan Shelley

. . . will help you to develop the crucial skill of being able to control your spending by living on a budget . . . reading this or one like it will help you to avoid putting strain your marriage from careless spending or too much debt (remember that money is the #1 reason that married couples argue)

It's Not About Me - Teen Edition by Max Lucado

. . . can help you to get your focus off of yourself and on to God and others (that's where the real joy is!)

"A life rule is a rule that you try to apply in every situation in your life. May I suggest the life rule of "Always Respect™." Respect your job/education, respect others by treating them with respect, and respect yourself by taking care of yourself. Using this life rule will help you to have joy."
(This quote as well as the information on pp. 119-123 are from RespectClub.org. Respect Club promotes respect in schools.)

The following information is for teens who prefer a description of the characteristics of a keeper in nonspiritual language (I replaced the words "a keeper" with the words "a strong person."):

The Five Qualities of a Strong Person ™

The Five Qualities of a Strong Person are:

- Character

- Attitude

- Responsibility

- Effort

- Self-control

Here are the qualities of a strong person in more detail:

Character (acronym = HIT)

- honesty - they don't lie, deceive, cheat or steal

- integrity - they do what they say they're going to do. In other words, they're a person of their word. A strong person, who one day gets married, almost always keeps their marriage commitment to love, honor, and cherish their husband or wife. This means that they don't cheat on their husband or wife, they try to meet their husband's or wife's emotional, physical, social, and financial needs, and they try to love their husband or wife in thought, word, and actions every day

- trustworthiness - they can be trusted in all situations

Attitude (acronym = CCFFHR)

- caring - they truly care about other people, they treat others in a caring manner

- cheerful - they try to be as cheerful as possible in all situations, they try to brighten the day of others

- friendly - they're willing to be a real friend to others (please see Chapter 5), including being willing to be a real friend to someone who's ignored or rejected by others

- forgiving - they're willing to forgive others who treat them with disrespect - even if the other person isn't sorry for what they've done

- helpful - they try to help others as much as possible because it's a good choice and because someday it's more than likely that they'll need help from someone

- respectful - they treat other people with respect, even people who don't treat them with respect and people who they don't like

Responsibility (acronym = HATS)

- for handling pains in a positive way (a pain is a person who you have trouble getting along with, who you don't like, and/or who has been mean to you)

- for always trying to make a good choice

- for taking care of themselves

- for serving others

Effort

A strong person gives their best effort in everything they do. They're known as a hard worker. They believe that anything worth doing is worth doing to their best ability. They take pride in the fact that they always try to do their best even when their best isn't as good as someone else's best (because everyone has different levels of ability and skills - and that's OK). They believe that giving their best effort will make it more likely that they'll be successful.

Self-Control (acronym = BATM)

- of their body

Way too many people don't know how to control their body by only using violence when absolutely necessary for self-defense. Since movies, TV, video games, and other things in our popular culture make using our bodies to hurt other people seem OK and even exciting - many people don't understand how important it is to be strong by being a man or a woman of peace and that violence is evil.

A person also needs to control their body sexually. To be honest, I don't believe that there's such a thing as "safe sex" before marriage - and the reason that I don't believe it is because I've seen, heard about, and read about the harm sex before marriage does to people. (please see Chapter 16)

- of their anger

First of all, let me clear up a fairy tale that I hear from my

121

students almost every day. They tell me that "so and so made me angry" and/or "I have an anger problem that I can't control." They don't seem to believe me at first when I explain to them that there's no such thing as someone else making them angry and that they can learn to control their anger if they really work at it. I try to prove this by saying, "Heaven forbid, but let's imagine that you've been in a car accident and you're lying in the hospital in a coma which means that you can't see and you can't hear because you're hurt so badly - and then a person who you say is 'making you angry' comes into the room and does the exact same thing that 'makes you angry' - would you have any reaction?" They say, "No, because I can't see or hear." I say, "That's right, when we're awake we take things in through our eyes, ears, and sense of touch and just like that, almost instantly, we make a bad choice in our minds to make ourselves angry. We turn our anger on just like a light switch - and we don't even realize it because we've flipped on the switch so many times before. Making ourselves angry is just a habit*.

So how does a person control their anger? The first step is to understand that we make ourselves angry as just described. The second step is to find ways to drain it every day without hurting yourself or others.

People drain their anger in different ways, for example:

- taking deep slow breaths

- counting to whatever number you need to count to in order to cool off and calm yourself

- going for a walk around the block

- exercising

- listening to music

- squeezing a stress ball

- going to their room to scream into a pillow

- going down to the basement to scream or yell (let people know what's going on so that they don't get scared) - some people find that it helps to also march in place while moving their arms and legs (like they're running) at the same time to release anger

- forgiving (not because the other person is sorry or because the other person deserves forgiveness, but because it helps you to get rid of your anger so that you don't become an angry person)

- of their tongue

- of their money

*Of course, not all anger is bad anger. Remember when Jesus flipped over the tables in the temple when the moneychangers had turned his Father's house into a den of thieves? A modern day example of righteous (good) anger is when a mother yells at her child who just ran into the street without looking both ways first. Righteous anger is anger with a good purpose - in this case, the purpose of helping her child learn the importance of crossing the street safely.

Ephesians chapter 4, verse 26 says: "Do not let the sun go down while you are still angry" (in other words, after everyone has had a chance to cool down, have a calm constructive caring discussion about the problem. Explain the reasons why you made yourself angry in a polite manner - please be sure to admit your mistakes and liberally apply forgiveness as needed).

True Love Lasts presentations - free on DVD

Until he kicks the bucket, the author is willing provide a free DVD of his 40-minute informational and somewhat humorous presentation about dating for church youth groups and Christian schools who are considering studying the book upon request. If your church or school would like a DVD, please send the name and address of your church/Christian school along with the name of your youth pastor/youth group leader/principal* via email to TLLinfo@aol.com. (*Their name is mentioned during the video.) Please include the approximate date that you plan to show the video. Also, please be sure to plan in advance, because it takes about 8 weeks for the digital copy to be mailed. (Of course, email addresses are never shared with anyone.)

Suggestions and Comments

Do you have a suggestion for a book that you would like to see added to the recommended books list in the Appendix? Want an additional chapter added to this book? Want a current chapter expanded? Find a typo? Have a suggestion for improving *Straight Talk About Teen Dating*? Do you have comments about the book that you'd like to share? If so, please email us at: TLLinfo@aol.com. Thank you!

True Love Lasts coming in 2014

The author plans to release a similar book to this one, rewritten and edited with a character emphasis (instead of with a Christian emphasis) for teens and young adults, entitled *True Love Lasts* in 2014.

How to become a Christian (if you're not one already)

"Every person can choose whether or not they'll spend eternity with God. The saddest thing on earth is that so many people choose not to."

The decision to become a Christian is without question the most important decision that a person will make in his or her life. You may have had a reaction when you read the last sentence. You may have said out loud or to yourself something like, "That's garbage!" - or something worse. You may have thrown down this book. I can understand your reaction especially if you're not being raised by parents who love Christ, if you've never experienced unconditional Christian love, or if you've had bad experiences with people who say they're a Christian. My request to you is that you keep reading with as open a mind as possible. Please take whatever time is needed to discover if becoming a Christian is garbage or if Jesus Christ told the truth when He said that whosoever believes in Him will have eternal life. You owe it to yourself to find out if Christianity is the truth or if it's a lie.*

My pastor, in one of his sermons said, "Christianity is inclusive, not exclusive." This means that anyone who wants to, regardless of what they've done in their life, can become a Christian. God will forgive you for whatever you've done if you turn to Him and decide to trust in Christ alone as your Savior. God promises eternal life to anyone who trusts in Christ alone as his or her Savior - it's a free gift from God, it cannot be earned, and there are no other requirements. So, what's a Savior anyway? A Savior is someone who saves someone from something horrible.

You may be asking the question, "Why do I need a Savior,

125

someone to save me - I haven't done anything really bad in my life?" The reason is that God is perfect and he doesn't let anyone who's not perfect into heaven. Do you know anyone who's perfect in thought, word, and actions? Me neither. That means that we're all sinners and the Bible says that we deserve to die because of our sin. (I know this sounds harsh - but that's what the Bible says - and no one in all of history has proven the important facts of the Bible to be wrong.)

And this death I'm talking about isn't just the death of your body. I'm talking about death as in being punished forever in hell. Many people don't believe that hell exists and many people don't believe that hell is a place of eternal torment.

Very sadly, they're wrong. Why do you think that the Bible, the handbook for living that God gave to us, mentions hell numerous times and warns us to take whatever action is necessary to avoid being thrown into hell? The reason is that hell is a real place, and since God loves us, He doesn't want us to end up there.

The good news is that God loves us so much that he sent his only Son to live on this earth over 2000 years ago and to die in our place on the cross. I realize that someone dying in your place is kind of hard to understand - so let me back up in time. In the years before Jesus Christ lived, a person had to bring animals and grain to be sacrificed on the altar of the Temple in order for their sins to be forgiven. Simply stated, their animals and/or grain would be placed on the altar, the High Priest would say a prayer asking God to transfer the sins of the person to the animals/grain.

Then the fire would consume that sacrifice and the sins of the person would be forgiven. It was as if their sins never existed. So, Jesus dying on the cross for you and for me was the sacrifice of all sacrifices. Why? - because he was perfect, he was and is the Son of God. He died on the cross as a sacrifice for the sins that you've committed so far in your life - and amazingly, for the sins that you'll commit today as well as during the rest of your life here on earth. He will only be this sacrifice for you if you decide to believe in Him and accept the gift of eternal life. In other words, *you'll live forever with God if you make the decision to trust in Christ alone as your Savior.*

You may be asking, "I'm confused about what it means to trust in Christ alone as your Savior." I know it's hard to relate to something that happened over 2000 years ago. Perhaps this story will help - let's imagine that your life is like driving an 18-wheel truck for the first time, with no training. At times you think you have things under control, things seem to be going pretty well, but truth be told you don't really know what you're doing. Probably sometime during your life you're going to have a crash - it might be a crash from a drinking problem, it may be a crash from a divorce, it may be a crash from losing your job, or from something else.

So, for the sake of moving this story along, let's say that your life does crash - in fact you crash your 18-wheel truck on a highway bridge, you know one of those bridges that goes over another highway. Your truck is lying on its side against the guardrail of the bridge and you're hanging from the cab door that opened from the impact of the wreck. You're looking down at solid concrete 100 feet below. Just then the engine bursts into flames. You're in deep trouble. You don't know what you're going to do.

It just so happens that a taxi is driving on the road underneath the bridge. The taxi driver looks up and notices you hanging from the cab door. He pulls his taxi off the road, jumps out, and runs into the middle of the road just below you. He knows that you're about to die. He decides that he's going to try to catch you. He yells up to you, "Let go - I'll catch you!"

You have a choice, you can either hold on to the cab door and be burned or you can trust that the Taxi Driver will catch you. Because the flames are coming closer and closer to you, and the Taxi Driver looks like he might be able to catch you, you decide to let go. You're falling, tumbling, falling - the Taxi Driver catches you, but your full weight crushes him. You escape with only bumps and bruises. The Taxi Driver, who broke your fall, has massive internal injuries and broken bones from your weight.

How would you feel about the Taxi Driver after he did this for you? Please think about it for a few seconds . . . . . I bet you would have some tender feelings toward him in your heart, feelings of gratitude, feelings of compassion, maybe even feelings of brotherly love. And I'm sure that you would visit him there in the hospital. And you are there - the Taxi Driver isn't doing very well. He's in bad shape; the Doctors can't seem to be able to stop all of the internal bleeding. He notices you out of the corner of his eye. You smile and ask how he's doing. He motions for you to come over to him. You walk over, bend down, and he whispers in your ear, "I want you to trust in Christ alone as your Savior and I want you to love other people" - then he closes his eyes and dies.

I bet that you'd remember those words the rest of your life. I bet that you'd trust in Christ alone as your Savior and that you'd do your best to love other people.

So, who does the Taxi Driver in the story represent? . . . . . That's right; the Taxi Driver represents Jesus Christ. We all have a choice, we can hold onto our life and live it selfishly without God - and be tormented in hell forever. Or we can let go, trust in Christ alone to save us, then try our best to live our life the way God wants us to - and live with Him forever. Just as the Taxi Driver died in your place in the story, Jesus Christ died in your place 2000 years ago on the cross. Remember the tender feelings that you had toward the Taxi Driver after he saved you? Do you have the same tender feelings toward Jesus Christ? Do you realize how much God truly loves you just the way you are? Do you realize that God wants you to trust in Christ alone as your Savior and that He wants you to love others?

You may be asking, "Is there anything else that you can tell me to explain what trusting in Christ alone as my Savior means?" Maybe this example will help: Imagine yourself sitting on a folding chair with your feet tucked under the chair so that no part of your body is touching the floor. At that point you're trusting in the chair alone to keep you from falling to the ground. Many people trust in a lot of things to try to earn their way to heaven - being a good person, doing good deeds, giving money to the church, etc. The problem is that being in heaven when your body dies can't be earned - it's a gift from God. In this example the chair represents Jesus Christ - if you trust in Christ alone as your Savior, you'll be with God forever.

The most important question of all is: Do you know if you die today that you'll be in heaven? It's great if you've made the decision to accept the gift of eternal life from God by trusting in Christ alone as your Savior. If not, my prayer is that very soon you'll get down on your knees and pray a prayer in your own words something like this: "Father in heaven, I admit that I have sinned many times in my life, please forgive me for my sins both in the past and in the future. I accept your gift of eternal life by placing all of my trust for getting to heaven in what Christ did for me on the cross. I'm trusting in Christ alone as my Savior. Help me to have a close relationship with you and to live my life in a way that would be pleasing to you. Amen."

If you've decided to trust in Christ alone as your Savior, God has sent his Holy Spirit to dwell inside of you - that's right God is living inside of you - how awesome is that! (see John, chapter

14, verse 16). You'll never be alone even if everyone here on earth abandons you. God will help you through whatever problems you have in your life. He doesn't promise us a problem free life, but He promises that He will help us through anything.

*Many people throughout history have questioned whether or not the Bible is true and whether or not Christ actually died on the cross for our sins. The greatest evidence that the Bible is true is the fact that hundreds of millions of peoples' lives have been changed for the good after they trusted in Christ alone as their Savior. A great short book to read about faith is Josh McDowell's *More than a Carpenter.*

Top 10 reasons why teens don't become a Christian:

10. They want to be in complete control of their own life (in other words, they want to do whatever they want to do whenever they feel like doing it)

9. They're more interested in personal gain and/or personal pleasure than living their life for Christ

8. They mistakenly think that the Christian lifestyle is boring

7. They fear rejection from their peers if they become a Christian and start living a Christian life

6. They don't want to be a "fanatic"

5. They think that all Christians are hypocrites because their actions don't always match what they say they believe (unfortunately Christians do have hypocritical behavior at times because everyone is sinful at times). With God's help, our responsibility is to show people through how we live our lives

that some Christians try very hard not to be a hypocrite.)

4. They've never been invited to attend youth group

3. They've never experienced unconditional Christian love

2. A Christian has never shared with them how Jesus Christ changed their life or explained to them how to become a Christian

1. They don't think they need Jesus Christ in order to be in heaven (They don't know or don't believe the words of Jesus recorded in John, chapter 14, verse 6.)

(If you feel that this information might be helpful to a friend who is not yet a Christian, please feel free to copy it and share it.)

Reflection: Have you made the decision to trust in Christ alone as your Savior and live your life for Him? If so, why? If not, why not? (Please talk over your questions and/or doubts with a strong Christian, your pastor, or your youth pastor.)

It's OK if you don't agree with everything in this book - please just use what made sense to help you to have a lifelong loving marriage (if you eventually decide to get married) and to live your life here on earth in such a way that when you arrive in heaven God will say, "Well done, good and faithful servant!"

131

About the Author

James Wegert has earned three college degrees, but he's learned the most from the School of Hard Knocks (making mistakes). He has years of professional experience working with teens and is certified as a school counselor for grades K-12. He also has experience as a volunteer Sunday School teacher and church youth group leader. Based upon this experience, he feels that many people don't have enough good information about dating from a Christian perspective before dating and during dating. He wrote *Straight Talk About Teen Dating* and *Straight Talk About Dating* (for ages 20+) in order to glorify God and to help reduce the divorce rate in our society. The author strongly feels that people can maximize the possibility that they'll have a lifelong loving Christian marriage if they put in the effort required to complete the journey of preparing themselves for dating.

"A keeper (a strong person) isn't overly concerned about what mean (weak) people say, do, or think - he or she knows that these things are out of his/her control."

"A person who is loving, caring, and giving - and who puts the needs of others first by getting off of themselves, is more likely to have the best possible life."

"Any goal worth going after (like becoming a keeper) is worth the work it's going to take to achieve it."

132

Bulk Order Form

"Save by ordering in bulk direct from the publisher"

Straight Talk About Teen Dating books*:

10-49 copies - $6.00** per copy with free shipping
50 copies and up - $5.00** per copy with free shipping

# of books requested_____   Cost_____

PA residents add 6% tax or include
a copy of your tax-exempt form   _____

                                                  Total _____

Please send your first name and last initial, shipping address, and check/money order (made payable to Strong Book Publishing - your information is never shared) to:

Strong Book Publishing
PO Box 5234
Lancaster, PA 17606-5234

*Single books can be purchased at your favorite bookseller.

**Prices are subject to change without notice. Please allow up to 3 weeks for delivery. If you have any questions, please email us at TLLinfo@aol.com. Thank you.

Made in United States
Troutdale, OR
12/08/2024

26089251R00087